100 Ideas for Primary Teachers:

Raising Boys' Achievement

Other titles in the 100 Ideas for Primary Teachers series

100 Ideas for Primary Teachers: Supporting Children with Dyslexia
by Gavin Reid and Shannon Green

100 Ideas for Primary Teachers: Behaviour Management
by Molly Potter

100 Ideas for Primary Teachers: Computing
by Steve Bunce

100 Ideas for Primary Teachers: Developing Thinking Skills
by Steve Bowkett

100 Ideas for Primary Teachers: Outstanding Teaching
by Stephen Lockyer

100 Ideas for Primary Teachers: Transition to Secondary School
by Molly Potter

100 Ideas for Primary Teachers:

Raising Boys' Achievement

Gary Wilson

B L O O M S B U R Y

LONDON · OXFORD · NEW YORK · NEW DELHI · SYDNEY

Bloomsbury Education
An imprint of Bloomsbury Publishing Plc

50 Bedford Square
London
WC1B 3DP
UK

1385 Broadway
New York
NY 10018
USA

www.bloomsbury.com

Bloomsbury is a registered trade mark of Bloomsbury Publishing Plc

First published 2016

British Library Cataloguing-in-Publication Data
A catalogue record for this book is available from the British Library.

ISBN

PB 9781472934451
ePub 9781472934475
ePDF 9781472934444

Library of Congress Cataloging-in-Publication Data
A catalog record for this book is available from the Library of Congress.

10 9 8 7 6 5 4 3 2 1

Typeset by Newgen Knowledge Works (P) Ltd., Chennai, India

Printed by CPI Group (UK) Ltd, Croydon, CR0 4YY

This book is produced using paper that is made from wood grown in
managed, sustainable forests. It is natural, renewable and recyclable. The
logging and manufacturing processes conform to the environmental
regulations of the country of origin.

To view more of our titles please visit www.bloomsbury.com

Many thanks as always for your love and inspiration
Zoe, Ben and Martha

Contents

Acknowledgements xi
Introduction xii
How to use this book xiii

Part 1: Boys and literacy 1
1 Reading at home 2
2 Reading at school 3
3 The power of persuasion 4
4 Why and what boys need to read 5
5 Engaging boys in reading fiction 6
6 Getting boys reading: We did it our way 7
7 Reading needs role models too! 8
8 I read this and I thought of you 9
9 Ban the book report 10
10 Speaking and listening: Getting it right
    from the start 11
11 Space for talking 12
12 What's all that noise about? 13
13 Speaking and listening: Tips for parents 14
14 Write from the start 1 16
15 Write from the start 2 17
16 Writing is exciting! 18
17 Writing with added boy appeal 19
18 Playing drama games 20
19 Role play into writing 1: The first steps 21
20 Role play into writing 2: Introducing
    characters 22
21 Mantle of the expert 1 23
22 Mantle of the expert 2 24
23 Purpose and audience 25
24 Multimodal literacy 26
25 Key points for boys and writing 1 28
26 Key points for boys and writing 2 29
27 Stimulating writing 1: Tried and tested
    ideas to get boys writing 30
28 Stimulating writing 2 32
29 Stimulating writing 3 33

Part 2: Developing emotionally intelligent boys **35**

30 Emotional intelligence: Self-awareness 36
31 Self-esteem and aspirations 37
32 Give responsibility and raise self-esteem 38
33 Building self-confidence one day at a time 39
34 Self-esteem wordle 40
35 Become totally incompetent: Raise
   self-esteem 41
36 What a juicy mistake 42
37 Praise 43
38 Praise postcards 44
39 Dealing with feelings 45
40 In the right state 46
41 Feeling good, working well 47
42 Peer massage 48
43 7% is the words that we use 49
44 Developing emotionally intelligent
   classrooms 50
45 Don't say a word! 51
46 The good news board 52
47 Celebrate! 53

Part 3: Teaching and learning **55**

48 Pushing all the right buttons 56
49 Switch on! 57
50 Switch on! Challenge! 58
51 Come along, it's your time you're wasting 59
52 Connect to their emotions 60
53 Activate the learning 61
54 Aw...do we have to write about it, Miss? 62
55 Stop mental truancy! 63

Part 4: Play **65**

56 But they don't know how to play! 66
57 Play more, learn more 67

Part 5: Parents need to know this stuff **69**

58 Parents need to know this stuff 1 70
59 Parents need to know this stuff 2 71
60 Parents need to know this stuff 3 72
61 Top tips for parents – Early Years 1 73
62 Top tips for parents – Early Years 2 74
63 Developing independence 75
64 Taking the pressure off 76
65 Top tips for parents 1 77
66 Top tips for parents 2 78

Part 6: Positive male role models   **79**

67 Positive male role models in the wider
community   80

68 Men behaving dadly 1   81

69 Men behaving dadly 2   82

70 FUDGE (Friends, uncles, dads, grandads,
everyone!)   83

71 Positive male role models in the school
community   84

Part 7: Gender stereotyping   **85**

72 Investigate and challenge gender stereotypes   86

73 Genderwatch! The way forward!   87

74 Gendered behaviour – the way forward for
teachers   88

75 Gender issues in school: take a health check   89

Part 8: Peer pressure   **91**

76 Peer pressure   92

77 Dealing with peer pressure   93

78 Dealing with the peer police 1   94

79 Dealing with the peer police 2 – go large!   96

Part 9: Labelling boys   **99**

80 We say the craziest things!   100

81 Positive labels   101

82 Labels really stick   102

83 Am I brilliant today or am I fantastic?   103

84 So what do you expect?   104

**Part 10: Getting boys on the agenda (a quick
strategic approach)**   **105**

85 Getting boys on the agenda 1   106

86 Getting boys on the agenda 2: Next steps   107

87 Let's hear it from the boys   108

88 So what do we know already?   109

89 Meeting 2: Barriers   110

90 Where do we go from here?   111

91 Staff meeting 3 continued   112

92 Staff meeting 3 continued   113

Part 11: Checklists and quick tips   **115**

93 A quick checklist for primary teachers in a hurry   116

94 Quick tips for teachers in a hurry   118

95 More quick tips for teachers in a hurry   119

Part 12: A few more words from the experts   **121**
96 Get it right for the boys 1   122
97 Get it right for the boys 2   123
98 We did it our way 1   124
99 We did it our way 2   126
100 Boys love teachers who . . .   128

Acknowledgements

I would like to thank:

Di Pumphrey - Head of School and Ruth Fitze - Communication and Thinking Leader at West Thornton Primary Academy

Adam Robbins, Assistant Headteacher, Richard Alibon Primary School
Fiona Bird
Rachel Wills at Saltburn Reading campus
Oxford University Press
The National Literacy Trust
The UKLA
Luke Abbott
Dorothy Heathcote
Gill Matthews and Stephanie Austwick
Helen Arya
Limeside Primary School
Armitage C of E Primary School
Shonette Bason
Lancashire SureStart

Jack, Harry and the hundreds of other boys I have spoken to over the last 23 years! And Kate for her patience and kindness.

Introduction

There is no single reason why some of our boys underachieve, nor is there a quick fix, but there are countless practical ideas that can help you to address the issue. This book is a collection of some of them.

I have long resisted the idea of presenting a book containing simply a collection of ideas that can be used to chip away at what is a complex problem: the underachievement of some of our boys. Just how complex this is I outline in great detail in *Breaking Through the Barriers to Boys' Achievement*. I have therefore slightly bent the rules by also including a number of simple strategic models, including ways of getting gender on the agenda in your school and getting parents on board from the very outset (see also *How to Help Your Boys Succeed*). It must always be at the forefront of our minds that the work to engage and motivate boys must never be to the detriment of girls. I have always maintained that anything we do that addresses the attitude, behaviour and subsequently the performance of boys will have a positive knock-on effect for girls. All the strategies here are ones that engage and motivate boys without disadvantaging girls. As you will discover in these pages, sometimes it can be a simple tweak and sometimes it means challenging one's own practice. Both of those elements are present here.

Never mind boys will be boys...boys will be brilliant!

How to use this book

This book includes quick, easy, practical ideas and guidance for you to dip in and out of to help you in raising boys' achievement.

Each idea includes:

- a catchy title, easy to refer to and share with your colleagues
- a quote from a practitioner, parent or child describing their experience that has led to the idea
- a summary of the idea in bold, making it easy to flick through the book and identify an idea you want to use at a glance
- a step-by-step guide to implementing the idea.

Each idea also includes one or more of the following:

Teaching tip

Practical tips and advice for how and how not to run the activity or put the idea into practice.

Taking it further

Ideas and advice for how to extend the idea or develop it further.

Bonus idea ★

There are 9 bonus ideas in this book that are extra-exciting, extra-original and extra-interesting.

Share how you use these ideas and find out what other practitioners have done using **#100ideas**.

Boys and literacy

Part 1

Reading at home

"Home and family are crucial in the development of reading and writing, particularly in terms of reading for pleasure." National Literacy Trust 2014.

All teachers know the importance of parental influence in reading, but recent studies suggest that only around half of younger children are read to at home. Quite a number may never be read to or see older males reading in the house, therefore they think that reading stories is a 'girlie' thing to do. We need to make sure that school encourages parents to read with their children right from the start.

Teaching Tip

Find advice for parents on helping their child's reading, including free eBooks, at www.oxfordowl.co.uk.

Taking it Further

Invite dads, granddads, uncles and older brothers in to talk about the importance of reading to them in their lives (at work and at leisure) and to read to the class some of their favourite children's stories.

Bonus Idea ★

Provide a list of, and lend out, books for boys to read to their younger siblings.

Here are some suggestions for how to encourage reading at home.

- Mount a display about reading at home in your classroom, including examples of books, pictures of parents reading to children (dads as well as mums) and advice in the form of labels, bullet lists or take-home leaflets.
- Keep advice for parents simple and effective by using a 'top tip of the week card'. For example: 'When he asks you to read the same story over and over again, keep going – at that precise moment, he is learning to read.'
- Display a mission poster in a prominent place saying 'We would love to see all of our children read to by all the adults in their home.'
- Set up 'dads and lads' reading groups.
- Establish a pupil and parents' 'Book of the Week' section to your school's website. Invite dads to fill in a simple proforma about the books they like reading with their boys and display the results: 'I thought ... was a fantastic read because ... and the best bits were ... I'd recommend it!'

Reading at school

"Readers will be leaders is what my teacher said!"

Show children that your school values reading (and keep track of the kinds of books that they like reading).

- Hold a reading week during which everybody (staff and children) reads a fiction book for forty minutes every day. Repeat every half term.
- Hold a reading challenge or provide a list of selected books that children can read over a term. Give bronze, silver or gold awards, or create an 'extreme reading' board (see Teaching Tip for more details).
- Create 'challenge' bookmarks listing a range of easier books to harder ones – the boys can tick them off as they read them.
- Display posters of cool male role models reading. These can be found on the National Literary Trust (NLT) or the American Library Association. Sportsmen are often a popular choice.
- Join the NLT's 'Reading Champions'.
- Hold bring-and-buy book sales to build stock.
- Display photos of staff reading, with captions saying why they chose that book.
- Hold a 'Match the Teacher' competition: display the teachers' favourite books, and ask children to work out which book goes with which teacher!
- Create book displays featuring favourite childhood reads of all male members of staff. Make sure to include everyone, from the caretakers to the governors.
- Shadow book awards and have your own judging and awards ceremonies.
- Hold inter-class reading challenges.
- Hold assemblies with a reading focus that involves pupils, teachers and parents.

Teaching Tip

Discuss with your colleagues: Which of these do we do, what others could we try? Then don't forget to ask the experts (the boys themselves) what would encourage them to read more.

Taking it Further

Hold an 'extreme reading' competition where pupils, staff and parents submit photographs of the strangest places they have read a book.

Bonus Idea

Suggest having family film nights based on popular books and encourage families to read the books together before or after the event.

The power of persuasion

"I'm not a passionate lover of maths but I spend a lot of time persuading them that I am!"

Share an enthusiasm for books. Are there books on display that scream out to be read by boys?

Taking it Further

Engage a small 'Reading Squad' or group of 'Reading Stars' to give you their opinions and fresh ideas.

How often have you heard from boys, 'It's boring', 'I'm not really into reading', 'I don't have time to read', 'It's faster to watch a movie'? Could it also be true that a tiny minority of teachers might share some of these opinions? Not being a massive reader of children's literature is not a problem – many teachers, and boys, will have no problem sharing their enthusiasm for books.

Consider the following.

- Do children walk into your classroom and immediately know that you love reading?
- Are your reading areas welcoming and organised spaces? (Remember, some boys need order and systems to function well).
- Do they see a passion for all things books? For example, posters, character puppets, and lively, interactive displays.
- Is the class library display as attractive as a bookshop?
- Do all children, boys and girls, see their interests reflected in the reading materials on display?
- Is there a wide variety of types of reading material on display, including comics, graphic novels, and electronic reading materials?

Review your classroom environment using these six questions as a checklist.

Why and what boys need to read

"It's only in fiction that boys will find the words to unclench their hearts."

Reading fiction is important for boys in many ways, not least because it encourages reflection.

Engaging boys in reading in school is important for a number of reasons.

- Girls tend to read more fiction (particularly in high schools) whilst there is a tendency for boys to read more non-fiction
- Non-fiction challenge levels tend to be higher than for fiction.
- Pupils who read a greater proportion of non-fiction make less reading progress than pupils who read a high proportion of fiction.

Boys need to read fiction because it helps them to develop emotional intelligence and the ability to reflect by:

- exposing them to a wide range of experiences, attitudes and people that mirror real life
- aiding their understanding of what others might be thinking and/or feeling, and why this might affect how they act
- encouraging them to identify with characters and their emotions, thereby helping them to understand their own emotions and those of others
- giving them strategies to deal with dilemmas and conflicts
- providing them with the words they need to express themselves.

Teaching Tip

Look for book trailers on YouTube together. Get pupils to make some themselves. What other ways of persuading boys that reading is a cool thing can *they* think of? They are the experts, remember!

Taking it Further

What things from the list in Idea 3 has anyone in school tried? What else could you try?

Engaging boys in reading fiction

"20% would read more if they knew what to read." National Literacy Trust 2014.

The best way to engage boys in reading is to introduce them to exciting books.

It is important to ensure that you are providing a range of fiction that has boy appeal. Of course, all boys are different and have different tastes, but most boys enjoy books that:

- appeal to their sense of mischief
- are funny
- are plot driven
- are written in a series
- have an edge to them
- are about powerful ideas
- draw on myth, legend and fantasy.

Here are some more practical ideas that you might try:

- a secret boys' book club
- a comic/graphic novel club
- a secret squad that post cryptic clues about new arrivals in the library
- a box of books in the library, padlocked to arouse curiosity
- reading response blogs
- dads, granddads and uncles reading ghost stories round a campfire as a PTA event
- dads, granddads and uncles invited in to read after family assemblies or after drop off time
- contact with authors via author websites.

Getting boys reading: We did it our way

"We're the reading squad and we love to read!"

West Thornton Primary School have developed a lively, thriving community of readers that engages all the boys and all the girls. Read through some of their list of actions to see which ones you can implement.

- From time to time have a 'wild read' (read outside).
- Have a free book exchange to normalise the idea of reading at home.
- Advocate sharing stories with the family.
- Hold 'reading + cake = pleasure' events.
- Write a never-ending story on a roll of wallpaper that everyone reads regularly.
- Have an annual 'book blowout festival'.
- Have a rent-a-reader scheme: 'Do you have a reader who loves...'.
- Have a 'thousand readers wall': a wall with photographs of 1000 readers on it!
- Have regular book sales.
- Advertise your reading: 'We are currently reading...'.
- Have a boy-friendly area in the library.
- Have older boys reading to younger boys in the school.
- Get involved with the NLT's 'Reading Champions'.
- Keep parents (particularly older males) behind after family assemblies to read to the children.
- Have regular public library visits.
- Have a group 'Guerrilla Poets'; poems can turn up anywhere, anytime for anyone to read!
- Have a 'Shelfie' project, where pupils can take pictures of themselves and their bookshelves with their favourite books.

Teaching Tip

Ask your boys what they think about some of these ideas. Find volunteers for a 'Reading Squad' to read to younger ones.

Taking it Further

Select some of your 'Reading Squad' to run masterclass sessions to show other boys how they could do it too.

Reading needs role models too!

"43% of readers are reading something as a result of peer recommendation." National Literacy Trust 2015.

If boys see other boys reading, they are more likely to think it is a worthwhile activity. Try some of these ideas in your school.

Teaching Tip

Encourage boys to recommend books that they've read to friends (friends' recommendations are special!). But have the rule 'no spoilers allowed in class!'

Taking it Further

Encourage Year 6 pupils to donate a book when they leave school and to write a 'bookplate' for it. A public end-of-term ceremony at which they officially donate the books, followed by a display in the school library, can have a strong impact.

- Ask your local high school to send boys, as well as girls, to carry out work experience. Train up the boys in how to read in order to engage and excite their young listeners.
- Ask Year 6 boys to help with reading in the Early Years. Encourage them to make it exciting, perhaps by presenting role plays based upon story books.
- Give your older boys books that have been shortlisted for the Carnegie Medal (picture books), and send them into Year 1 to read and discuss the stories with younger boys.
- Invite older males from the community to come in and read a favourite story from their childhood, and/or to talk about the importance of reading in their lives for pleasure and for work. (The NLT's Reading Champions scheme has many more ideas for presenting older male role models as readers).

I read this and I thought of you

"If they can read but they don't have a passion for it then we have failed. Showing them that we are passionate about reading ourselves can really help."

Having a wide range of books for a variety of purposes can really help.

There is a considerable amount of research to suggest that children reading to themselves makes a marked difference in their development as readers.

Their silent reading time is a precious time, and an opportunity to demonstrate that you're a passionate reader by quietly engaging with students one-on-one about what they're reading, and discuss what they enjoy about their chosen book.

If you have space in your classroom, try the three-library approach.

- Teacher's library: your own collection of favourite children's books, from which you can hand a 'special' book to a reluctant reader with the magic words 'I thought of you when I read this, you can borrow it if you like.'
- The class library: where children make their own choices. Ensure that choosing a new book is not part of 'reading time'.
- The enquiry library: an easy to use reference library that includes computer hardware and appropriate software, with a regularly refreshed list of useful authors' websites and book reviews.

Teaching Tip

Engage boys and girls in selecting books from school bookfairs for the class or school library.

Taking it Further

Invite pupils to write short reviews of the books they have read and put them on Amazon. The fact that these reviews may be read across the world is a great motivator, in much the same way as Pobble (described in Idea 17) provides a very powerful experience of writing for and receiving comments from readers all over the world.

Ban the book report

"I like reading, but why do we always have to write about it after?"

Talking about reading suits boys better than having to write about it every single time.

Taking it Further

Invite boys to stand up in assembly and talk about books that excite them. Target peer leaders. As we will see in Idea 76 this can be particularly powerful.

As the title implies, *Ban the Book Report: Promoting Frequent and Enthusiastic Reading* by Graham Foster talks about the fact that having to write about absolutely everything they read can take the enthusiasm away from the reader, as they always know there's a catch coming at the end! What's more, this makes reading even less appealing for those who are struggling with their writing.

Talking about their reading in a positive and enthusiastic way is a far more beneficial activity.

You can also invite them to act out scenes from the book with friends to encourage others to read, or create a short poem or piece of rap to extol the virtues of the book.

Engaging a boys' 'Reading Squad' in a special fact-finding mission into the appeal of reading and researching reading habits can be a useful approach. For example, they could analyse Junior Librarian statistics for boys' favourite books and reading patterns and ask all pupils how many books they read, their favourite genre, what recommendations they have, whether they get books for presents, etc.

Speaking and listening: Getting it right from the start

"Research suggests that girls use between ten and thirty times as much language as boys in their early play."

It is generally understood that girls are more advanced than boys in speaking and listening in their early years. If we want to raise boys' achievement, it is of vital importance to create a language-rich environment in school (during lessons and playtime) and in the home.

The following approaches are particularly useful to maximise the development of language.

- Relate talk to the immediate context and help the child to explore the topic further.
- Talk with the child, not at him; be a genuine language partner.
- Be patient. Listen with genuine interest to what the child has to say, and hand conversation back to him. Don't leap in with an answer.
- Don't overload conversation – when a child gives a word or short sentence, respond by restating, extending and expanding slightly on what he says.
- Give personal contributions, such as, 'I had a surprise too. Yesterday my...'
- Don't cross-examine; instead give an alternative. 'Are they blue or red?' is more helpful than open or 'test' questions.
- Avoid correcting, interrupting, or asking a child to repeat words; instead restate what the child is trying to say, aiming for meaning rather than correct language.
- Have a bag with a few objects in it. When a child chooses an object they say the word, e.g. 'train'. Then demonstrate putting the word into a sentence, e.g. 'Yes, it is a black train.' This encourages children to start thinking and speaking in complete sentences.

Adapted from work by Webster, 1987.

Teaching Tip

Make that leap into what's going on in a boy's head, in a boy's world, in a boy's universe! Superheroes are a great place to start. Instead of a home corner or baby clinic, let's have a superhero den! (Great for girls too, of course. There are lots of female superheroes and we could do with more!)

Space for talking

"Can we have us tea round the table mam, go on mam, can we have us tea round the table like they do on *The Simpsons*?"

It is true to say that there are children from low-income families all over the country who can't string a sentence together when they start school, who think their name is 'son' because they never get called by their name. The need to focus on presenting opportunities for developing speaking and listening skills, for boys in particular, is clearly evident.

Teaching Tip

What other spaces have you created as a group of staff? What have you noticed about the effectiveness of these spaces? Share positive and negative experiences of the spaces you have created. What other spaces might you consider creating now?

Less than half the homes in the UK now have tables around which families eat and talk. It is interesting to note that in France, Spain and Italy, for example, the development of speaking and listening skills is relatively trouble free, but then there are elements of those cultures, most notably family mealtimes, which remain sacrosanct.

Elizabeth Jarman's work on places for boys to talk, particularly in Early Years, suggests a very rich and varied range of settings with a very specific focus in each.

- Places to enjoy books that are essentially cosy areas, with lots of related props and figures.
- A place for group negotiation containing, for example, 20 flat packed boxes.
- Secret spaces to retreat to and reflect, such as dens or pop-up tents.
- Places to build, where the language they use will be rich and full of estimating, planning and reflecting.
- Secret spaces, e.g. long grass with a path cut through it and small open spaces at various intervals.

What's all that noise about?

"They spend as much time in the playground as they do in literacy."

Playtime and lunchtime provide the ideal opportunity to develop creative speaking and listening activities. With your staff, share ideas and discuss ways to promote creative play.

Case study: Scrapstore playpod

Warwick University researched the amount of creative language used in six primary school playgrounds. First, they identified the most common piece of play equipment found in the six schools: the 'trim trail'. They found over any given lunchtime the trail was taken up less than 10% of the time, with very little creative language used.

Next, they introduced a 'scrapstore playpod' into the playgrounds; placing 1500 pieces of safe scrap, including items such as tyres and old telephones inside a large shed-like container. They then invited children to explore! The effect was remarkable. The take up was, on average, over 90% over the term, and many children were engaged in co-operative role play for the entire lunch break. Teachers noted that boys in particular were in a far better state for learning in the afternoon.

I mentioned this approach during a primary school visit. Next time I visited, I was greeted by a stern-looking caretaker. 'Ah! You're back! Come with me,' he ordered. 'Look at this! That's your blooming fault that is!' With a grin, he indicated a car, minus windows, sitting slap bang in the middle of the playground.

Teaching Tip

You might want to start small scale, with a collection of items that could be used for role play in the playground.

Taking it Further

Develop a stage or performance area in the playground, or provide a beautifully ornate storytelling chair.

Speaking and listening: Tips for parents

"If you stop answering his questions he will stop asking them!"

Some ideas to help families to help their boys develop speaking and listening skills.

- Enjoy reading, reciting and singing rhymes and songs together.
- Discuss the pictures, and use props such as character-related toys or wizards' hats.
- Use funny voices for the different characters when you read.
- Make up your own stories together. Try this approach, based on the excellent work devised by educator Pie Corbett (Storymaking and Talk for Writing):

  ° Imitate: Tell a story that you both know – making it even more fun by incorporating actions
  ° Innovate: Tell it again, but add a new twist (perhaps you could bring yourselves into the story!)
  ° Invent: Tell a new story, but use the same basic structure as the story you started with.

- Ask grandad, or other relatives (especially if they live some distance away), to make a CD of stories. This could be favourite stories or stories about themselves when they were children.
- When you are out and about, point out things you see around you, and talk about them.
- Eat together as regularly as you can, and share your thoughts and feelings about the day.
- Wash up together!
- Talk as you do jobs around the house together (this is sometimes the best time for boys to talk about their concerns and problems!).

- At bedtime, chatting about the day as well as reading bedtime stories.
- Talk 'with' him, not 'at' him.
- Look at your boy when you talk with him – it shows him he's valued.
- Have fun together!
- Play imaginative games together. Develop characters' voices as you play and encourage your boy to do the same. The more excited and involved you are, the chattier and more engaged he will become.
- Play board games together.

Adapted from *How to Help your Boys Succeed – The Essential Parents' Guide,* G. Wilson, Bloomsbury Publishing PLC.

Write from the start 1

"The difficulties that many boys find with writing at foundation stage is an early taste of failure that many never recover from."

In assessments of physical development (and virtually everything else) in the Early Years/Foundation Stage, girls consistently outperform boys.

Teaching Tip

Explore resources such as *Write Dance*, which can be extremely useful as it is engaging, fun and helps develop gross and fine motor skills.

In Early Years it is widely understood that boys' fine motor skills tend to develop at a slower pace than girls'. The fact that many boys have difficulties with their handwriting throughout school is not their fault, and boys tend to lose self-esteem and confidence when adults over-emphasise the importance of neat work. It's important that adults, both teachers and carers, show understanding, and help boys develop their fine motor skills.

All Early Years' activities should help boys develop their fine motor skills, and can be adapted to do so.

Climbing and crawling

Provide:

- low level climbing activities, including planks to walk across
- open cardboard boxes to crawl through.

Making patterns and shapes

Provide:

- decorating brushes and buckets of water to 'paint' the walls and fences
- scarves and ribbons to throw and catch, and to make patterns by twirling
- a thin layer of sand, cous cous or shaving foam in a shallow tray to make patterns and shapes using the index finger
- squeezy bottles filled with liquid to make patterns on the ground.

Bonus Idea ★

If your school takes on board peer massage (see Idea 42) then this will be another daily activity to help develop fine motor skills.

Write from the start 2

"Just stop fiddling, put that down and listen to me!"

How often have you heard yourself say that? Unfortunately, if he does put it down, he may stop listening to you as well — because it was helping him to focus *and* continuing to help develop his fine motor skills.

As discussed in Write from the start, development of fine motor skills is a key area of development, particularly for boys, at Foundation Stage. It is important to provide support and understanding to ensure they are confident, and do not feel a sense of failure. Most important, however, is lots of work from pre-school onwards on developing fine motor skills. Provide:

- dried beans, pasta, lentils, and rice for them to sort into different containers — encourage them to transfer objects using a spoon, tweezers or index finger and thumb
- a selection of plastic jars with screw top lids, and keys and padlocks
- buttons to drop into a jar
- dough to roll, cut pound and pinch
- cornflour 'gloop' to lift, stir and drip
- tubes cut into pieces, to thread onto doweling or plastic washing line
- elastic material squares to pull and squashy balls to squeeze
- newspaper and tissue paper to scrunch, and bubble wrap to pop.

Teaching Tip

Have a box of tricks on the table all the way through primary: lumps of playdough, blue tack, pipe cleaners, stress balls.

Investigate 'Dough Disco' (Shonette Basson) on YouTube

Taking it Further

These kinds of activities don't need to be restricted to primary years, of course. They can also be helpful for older boys. Boys often complain that their hands hurt after writing. In one high school in Derbyshire, boys were encouraged to carefully scrunch up paper and straighten it out using only one hand before they sat down to do a long written assignment. They found that this prevented their hands from aching during or after the set task.

Writing is exciting!

"If we fire up our imaginations we can ignite theirs."

If we make it dull then so will they!

Teaching Tip

What situations, surprises, weird happenings and strange events could you create that would fire their imagination? Make it memorable!

We can get boys really excited about writing in Early Years, but gradually it becomes harder to persuade some boys that writing is a good idea. The constant need for written evidence certainly don't help. But *we* can. Here are some ideas.

- A teacher in one school took the class to a butterfly house. Each member of the class was given their own caterpillar eggs to care for and write about. They wrote observations, explanations, recounts, and stories about butterflies.
- During a pond life project, one teacher engaged the boys by getting them to imagine they had shrunk to a miniscule size, and were exploring the pond in a tiny submarine: 'The water louse lashed out with its mighty claws, pulverising the flank of the submarine with one devastating swing.' Such thought experiments can have far-reaching consequences: it was as a result of Einstein imagining himself chasing a beam of light that he came up with the theory of relativity!

Taking it Further

Sometimes boys can be swept along by a teacher's energy and enthusiasm for a project and produce an amazing piece of writing, quite unlike anything they have produced before. That's your starting point, because if they've done it once then they can definitely do it again! At this point we raise our expectations of those boys.

- Another teacher, looking at William Buckingham's Snorgan sailor, built the mammoth's house in the field one school holiday and started the whole adventure by saying there had been reports of a large creature in the woods nearby. The idea of writing stories about the mammoth was so exciting that the boys in the class were happy to suspend their disbelief and engage in the story.

Writing with added boy appeal

"If they can't see a sense and purpose in doing something they won't blooming well do it."

Having a real audience for their writing really helps, as it makes more sense as far as a boy is concerned.

One of the most significant issues for boys when it comes to writing is motivation. As far as many boys are concerned, if they can't see a sense and purpose in doing something then they just won't do it. Or at least they won't do it to the best of their ability, and writing is a particular case in point. Sometimes simple works best.

- 'Pobble' is a website that allows you to publish children's work internationally and for free.
- Get the Year 6 boys to write stories for Year 1 pupils, and include copies of them in the class library.
- Produce a real newspaper in a day, using rolling news on television and news websites.

Boys will, of course, suspend their disbelief if they are enjoying what they are doing, for example:

- writing a letter to the headteacher's kidnappers trying to persuade them to let them go.
- writing to a favourite footballer criticising a recent performance and giving him advice about how he might improve.

Taking it Further

Explore the possibility of engaging with Pobble (formerly Lend Me Your Literacy), a free website which enables children to reach a worldwide audience. Pobble was started by a group of teachers in Harrogate. A member of the group told me a typical success story of a couple of boys who wrote a story together and uploaded it to the site. The next day 704 people around the world had read the story, more than a couple of hundred had 'liked ' it and about 70 were now going to 'follow' them, eager to read their next piece. Brilliant!

Playing drama games

"Boys need to know three things. Who's in charge? What are the rules? And, are they being applied consistently?" Sue Palmer

When playing games, boys need boundaries. If they don't have boundaries they can fly off in all kinds of directions.

Teaching Tip

Before you begin drama games, sit down and discuss with children what rules they think will be useful. They will probably mention one or two of the above list themselves. Then introduce the above to show how closely they reflect their own ideas.

- Have any resources you will need to play the game ready and at hand.
- When playing for the first time, have the instructions written in clear logical stages.
- Never start until children are still and silent.
- When giving instructions to the very young, keep them short and give them one at a time.
- Have clear and consistent verbal signals for starting and stopping a game and make sure they're understood.
- Have a range of strategies for obtaining silence that avoid you having to raise your voice (see Idea 45).
- Explain that they will sometimes choose for themselves who they work with and sometimes you will choose.
- If you fear they won't work well together try 'Choose a partner... now choose a different partner' before you start the game.
- Make sure they understand the limits of their own space and do not intrude on the space of other groups.
- Present rules and skills as challenges.
- Always look for opportunities to praise. If you have high but realistic expectations they will learn to respect your praise, so don't offer it if it isn't deserved.
- If some children are spoiling the game for others don't let the game continue, but don't make the whole class suffer.

Adapted from *Beginning Drama 4–11*, J. Winston and M. Tandy, David Fulton.

Role play into writing 1: The first steps

"I know the words now, I know what to write."

It is widely understood that role play is not only popular with boys but also a very powerful way to help develop writing.

It can be difficult to let go of the normal boundaries of the classroom. It helps to know that boys love role play. There are numerous warm up games and exercises that can be used to get children in the right frame of mind. The following and more can be found in *100+ Ideas for Drama* by Anna Scher and Charles Verrall (Heinemann).

- Word tennis: partners shout out names in a given category until one runs out of ideas.
- Thirty seconds please: One child talks for thirty seconds without hesitating. If they do, another person can challenge and carry on until the thirty seconds is up.
- Yes/no: One child answers questions for a minute without saying or gesturing yes or no.
- Speakeasy chair: Each child in turn is interviewed and says as much as they can about what they would do if they won a fortune, became someone famous, etc.
- Using three props (e.g. phone, hat, walking stick) the children take turns to act out a short story.
- A child reads out an imaginary letter they have received, or answers an imaginary phone call.
- In pairs, two children make friends, then, on a given signal, start arguing, then repeat.
- A story is told in a group with each participant ending their section with 'unfortunately' and the next ending theirs with 'fortunately', etc.

Teaching Tip

Hot seat characters before writing about them in a story. For example, before writing about pirates, hot seat the pirates in turn: 'When did you decide to become a pirate?', 'What did your parents think?', 'What is the most dangerous thing you've ever done?', 'What advice would you give to someone wanting to become a pirate?'

Role play into writing 2: Introducing characters

"Ssssh, I can hear a noise downstairs...who could it be?"

Role playing a character can be a really useful first step for boys to help develop characters for writing.

Taking it Further

More situation drama In small groups, get children to enact a situation by giving them random slips of paper with character names, location, time of day and a secret known only to them.

Here are some simple, tried and tested exercises to get them thinking about, behaving and talking like a variety of characters.

- **Waxworks** Children walk around the room and, on a given signal followed immediately by an instruction, they adopt a pose, e.g. 'Freeze! A teacher!' (always interesting this one – note the boys' responses compared to the girls'!).
- **Waxworks alive** After several changes of character, give the instruction to 'unfreeze' and begin a conversation in character with the person nearest to them.
- **People meet people** In small groups, enact a TV programme where each child in turn is asked questions by the audience about their childhood, their childhood ambitions, what they do, how they became famous and their ambitions for the future.
- **Props and characters 1** In pairs, each child picks a hat and then they begin a two character dialogue.
- **Props and characters 2** Each child picks a bag or glasses, mask, etc. and improvises on their own, then with a partner or in a small group.
- **Situation drama** Present a small group with a title on which to base a piece of drama, e.g. 'The door into the future', 'The last survivors'.

Mantle of the expert 1

"I love doing it, but I don't know what's happened to literacy!"

Seeing a clear sense and purpose to writing will be the signal for boys to engage.

'The Mantle of the Expert' is a process devised by the drama teacher and educationalist Dorothy Heathcote in the 1970s. It is, in effect, a whole-class role play that takes place over a period of time (for several weeks, if appropriate) and is well known to engage and excite the imagination of boys in particular. Here's how it goes.

- The class transforms itself into, for example, a transport company, space station, a newspaper office, etc., whatever fits with your current work.
- The children are then divided into different areas of expertise, such as transport planners, design team, research team, management team, etc.
- The tasks for each day are determined by the post/emails/bulletins the company receives (all supplied by the teacher of course!).
- All groups are involved at all times, and interactions between groups is incorporated in the planning to maximise engagement and interaction.

Taking the notion of whole-class role play and extending it into the 'Mantle of the Expert' approach has helped countless teachers create language-rich learning environments that have engaged and excited so many boys and girls. One particular benefit is that it provides a very clear sense and purpose to all the activity, be it speaking, listening or writing. What's more, they're 'doing' literacy without even knowing they are.

Teaching Tip

Plan a simple piece of whole-class role play as a 'taster' for a full blown 'Mantle of the Expert' project. For example, a court case where you are trying the witches for the death of Macbeth.

Taking it Further

Find out more and look at case studies by looking up 'Mantle of the Expert' on the internet.

Mantle of the expert 2

"They're more than happy to suspend their disbelief if they're enjoying themselves."

Really engage your boys by transforming your classroom into an exciting environment where adventures are created.

'Mantle of the Expert' projects typically involve transforming classrooms into communal World War II air raid shelters, travel agencies, an archaeological dig and so on. Using the 'Mantle of the Expert' approach has also resulted in classes developing themselves into enterprises such as television companies, historical researchers, park designers, etc. Dorothy Heathcote, the inventor of this approach, explains the core elements as follows.

- The learners take on responsibility for running an enterprise in a fictional world.
- The learners care enough about the goals of a fictional client that they engage in activities through which they begin to imagine the fictional world.
- Learners and teacher together: a) interact predominantly as themselves, b) imagine that they are experts who run the enterprise, c) imagine they are interacting as other people in the fictional world with whom the experts are concerned.
- Over time, the pupils engage in activities that at are both curriculum tasks, and professional practises in the fictional enterprise.
- The teacher must share power to position learners as knowledgeable colleagues and ensure that they do the same.
- The learners must reflect to make meaning.

D.Heathcote 2006

Purpose and audience

"Have we got any letters back yet miss?"

Writing with a real purpose and audience is probably the most effective type of writing task that will engage boys.

This is an account of a piece of successful work by a class of 30 Year 6 children that the boys and girls found really exciting.

At the start of the year, the children wrote to people who inspired them: Stephen Hawking, Barack Obama, J.K. Rowling, footballers. One pupil, who supports a particular football club, had a very disappointing response to his letter, whereas a fan of another club was extremely pleased with the response to his. This led to the idea of investigating how each Premier League club treats their fans.

The children wrote to all 20 Premier League clubs. The letter asked questions about management style, player motivation etc. It was signed by an invented class member, Sam Fisher McCoy, and the only thing that changed was the manager and player names.

They evaluated each club response. Was it personal? Did they answer the questions? Did they send any photos? Every day, the children pestered their teacher – 'Have we got any letters?'

They have been featured in the local press, had a letter in local newspapers, the Sunday Times, Daily Mirror online, Twitter, Facebook. Look up 'Saltburn Primary League of Letters' on the internet and you will see the story.

The Premier League then contacted the class to say that their writing project is on the agenda at one of their meetings, to encourage clubs to engage with young supporters.

> **Teaching Tip**
>
> The teacher has used this approach most successfully at the beginning of term. Try it yourself! (Although Premiership football clubs might become less forthcoming if everyone writes to them!)

Multimodal literacy

"This is great, I know what to write now!"

The chief aim of the multimodal literacy kit is to support teachers and carers in working together to stimulate learning by increasing children's engagement with a wider range of texts.

Teaching Tip

Get children to keep a diary for a few days and stick memorable items like tickets inside, use a comic style format to tell a joke and gauge reaction of a reader, use a camera to take action shots and shots from different angles – consider the impact of close up shots taken to show emotions and the use of distant shots for settings, create an information text using a talking photo album to show facts on historical events, retell a favourite film in the style of one of the graphic books in the kit, create a scrapbook using the talking photobook to tell a personal adventure, write a diary for Hugo using information and facts from the story and ideas from *My Secret War Diary*, or write a spy diary for Alex Rider based on his adventure in the first assignment.

A work with the basic premise 'many texts that children enjoy outside the classroom are multimodal, combining the modes of sound, word, image and movement'. These materials were developed by looked-after children, but are suitable for the whole class, and developing the literacy curriculum. They've been proven to be particularly engaging for boys. A kit will need the following.

Multimodal texts Texts that present information in a variety of ways. In *The Invention of Hugo Cabret*, for example, huge sections of the story are told through illustrations alone. *My Secret War Diary* contains scribbled notes, diary pages, postcards, and so on.

Support books Books by members of the multimodal research team that contain more materials, ideas and activities.

I Know What to Write Now! Engaging Boys (and Girls) Through a Multimodal Approach by P. Bhojwani, B. Lord and C. Wilkes

Making Books by P. Johnson

Resources A rich variety of resources for recording, filming and illustrating their work will encourage children to engage creatively with the task. Choosing ways to present their ideas will help them to work from their own strengths.

For example, digital camera, talking photo album, headphones and microphones, memory stick, leaflets, non-permanent marker pens, graphic story grid examples, Hugo Cabret DVD, sketching pencils.

Choosing a format Each pupil needs to select which approach inspires them, or they may decide to combine some of the techniques from all three books.

These three graphic novels have been created in different formats:

- *Stormbreaker* – comic strip style text
- *The Invention of Hugo Cabret* – pages of pictures used to tell significant parts to the story as well as the printed word
- *My Secret War Diary* – scrapbook format with texts within a text.

Understanding graphic text Watch *The Invention of Hugo Cabret* film and note the use of camera shots. Several of the pictures in the book version have a film frame quality; see if children recognise some of the shots and consider the possible impact on the viewer. Which version do you prefer and why?

Taking it Further

See the teacher resource book in the kit entitled 'I know what to write now!' at ukla.org/publications: https://ukla.org/shop/details/i_know_what_to_write_now_engaging_boys_and_girls_through_a_multimodal_

Key points for boys and writing 1

"How come when we know boys have fantastic ideas we can't get them to commit them to paper?"

For the boys that we are concerned about when it comes to writing, there are some key points that will help.

Teaching Tip

Don't take my word for it; ask the boys what helps them with their writing. They are bound to add more to the list because they are the real experts.

Purpose Without a clear sense of purpose, many boys will not fully engage with the writing process.

Audience From writing stories for younger children to letters to authors, from writing book reviews for Amazon to writing for the whole world to see on Pobble (see Idea 17), boys will very often respond more readily if there is a clear audience.

Rehearse orally Many boys need the opportunity to role play, discuss or debate, argue, hot seat, conscience alley or forum theatre their ideas first before they put pen to paper. Until they've rehearsed something orally, they often can't write anything down.

Do we need to write it down this time? How often do we hear ourselves say, 'That was a great discussion, but now we need to get on with some work'? In effect, this discounts the value of speaking and listening activities. Do they really need to write it down on every occasion? How often do you notice some boys starting to lose interest towards the end of the session, because they know there's a catch coming?

Taking it Further

If you haven't already, then look at the work of Pie Corbett, particularly his work on storymaking and talk for writing.

Key points for boys and writing 2

"I like it that we can write things in different ways and sometimes we don't even have to write it down at all."

Quality oral feedback backed up by effective written feedback is vitally important, as children need to know exactly how they can improve.

Modelling writing There is no substitute for modelling writing for a particular group on a particular day for a particular purpose and focus. One of the most useful tools in a teacher's toolkit today is undoubtedly the visualiser. Can I share this with the rest of the class Errol?' 'No.' 'Can I pop it under the visualiser?' 'Yes!'

Allowing choice Where possible, give boys a choice of formats for their writing activity. This has been known to increase motivation and quality of outcome. By doing this, we allow them to work from their strengths and to take the lead in their own learning.

Chunk it Boys often work better with short-term goals and targets. Can the piece of work be 'chunked'? For example, a descriptive opening paragraph, a paragraph introducing a character, etc.

Feedback Show boys that sometimes we value quality over quantity, content over presentation. To constantly focus on the way it looks can have a hugely negative impact.

Celebrate their achievements Is there a culture in school that allows boys to celebrate their achievement (see Idea 47) or have the peer police taken their toll?

For more detail see *Breaking Through Barriers and Creating a Caring Masculinity*, G. Wilson, Bloomsbury Publishing PLC.

Teaching Tip

Mind maps are particularly useful for boys as they allow them to see the big picture. If they don't know how to use them then Tony Buzan's *Mindmapping for Kids* is a useful point of reference. Get children to plan out their next story or piece of writing using a mind map. They may even like to produce a mind map with a friend.

Taking it Further

Get children to write a story in 50 words or 120 characters. Boys like the challenge.

Stimulating writing 1: Tried and tested ideas to get boys writing

"We need to make that link to what's going on in a boy's head, in a boy's world, in a boy's universe."

We need to share ideas more. There are great ideas out there we need to pass on. The following are tried and tested ideas and resources that make writing tasks more appealing to boys.

- Use fabulous picture books as stimulus, e.g. *The Lost Thing* by S. Tan, *Flotsam* by D. Wiesner, *The Fantastic Flying Books of Morris Lessman* by W. E. Joyce, *How to Train Your Dragon* by C. Cowell, and the film of the same name.
- Use picture books with challenging ideas, e.g. *Erika's Story* by R. Vander Zee.
- Insert text/dialogue written on post-its into picture books without text.
- Use a multimodal approach (see Idea 23).
- Gather a series of natural objects on a walk in the woods and then challenge the children to write a story effectively incorporating them.
- Use visual story starters, e.g. a photograph inside an old mansion, edited to create a blank space for writing.
- Use actual CCTV footage of non-violent crime, write police reports and put all events together.
- Get children to create 'choose your own adventure' books (these were popular many years ago and are now beginning to reappear) using PowerPoint, with their own hyperlinks so that a reader can decide which way they want the story to go.

- Have a 'No pens day Wednesday'.
- Investigate Floor Books from Mindstretchers.
- Use talking photo albums.
- Look up software such as 'Comic Life', 'Puppet Pals', 'Toontastic', 'Animation Factory' and the work of Tim Rylands on 'ICT to Inspire'. There are many more ideas on The Literacy Shed website.
- Use iPad apps including 'Dragon Detector', 'Epic Citadel'
- Make your own books. See *Making Books* by P. Johnson.

Stimulating writing 2

"Do you remember that worksheet we did in January 2016?"

Make it memorable. Create irresistible learning with stunning starts and gripping ideas. Here is some inspiration.

Create artificial dilemmas and give them the problem to solve through investigations, interviews and reports. For example, there's been an invasion of the classroom overnight by frogs! Water and lilipads are strewn everywhere.

- Minibeast recipes: Collect 'food' (leaves, mud, etc.) then feed to minibeast of choice!
- Playscript versions of a Greek myth, with four scripts chosen to be acted out, directed by the writer, filmed and then shown to parents at a 'film premier' (red carpet, seating plan etc.) followed by a Q&A with the cast and director and an Oscar ceremony, with awards voted for by the class.
- UNICEF 'Day of Change' piece of whole-school writing based on emergency situations, such as a hurricane hitting the school so all the teachers wear high visibility jackets, the school is cordoned off and the power is shut down.
- Plan an international food festival, writing up recipes and methods from home. Advertise it with posters and invitation letters, each individually written by children and posted home. Create a recipe book and use the event for fundraising.
- Create a story, real or imagined, from a series of children's own family snapshots from home.
- Write a letter to mum and dad and go out with the class to post it at the local post office. (One Year 3 boy told me this was the best thing he's ever ever done!)
- Write on post-it notes and clipboards – it doesn't feel like writing.
- Incidental writing works well – in the middle of a discussion say, 'hmm, I think we need to make a list.' You don't even have to mention the 'W' word!

Stimulating writing 3

"I used to be a maths sort of person but now, when my teacher says it's literacy, I get that tingling feeling!"

'Writing for Real' is an approach to engaging children in writing, championed by Gill Matthews and Stephanie Austwick, that boys are particularly keen to engage with.

The key elements of boy-friendly writing are all there:

- something interesting and relevant to write about
- a context for their writing
- a purpose for their writing
- an authentic audience for their writing
- an engaging and motivating experience.

Idea 1 A special delivery arrives from an author – a mysterious package or small suitcase, containing another package and a letter which the teacher opens and reads, surrounded by the class who are in a heightened state of excited anticipation. 'Dear Class 5, I understand from your teacher that you are brilliant at coming up with ideas for stories. You may have read some of my children's books. My name is [insert appropriate author here]. The thing is, I need your help. I am desperately trying to come up with new ideas for a story. And by the way, I have sent you a present: copies of all my books!' At which point the excited class are all given copies to discuss with their groups and plan ideas for the author.

Idea 2 Actors from a theatre company burst into the classroom, shouting 'Don't be alarmed, but an alien has landed in the playground!' The children are led into the playground to see for themselves.

Teaching Tip

Unbelievably, a bottle with a message in it is found in your school pond. Maybe it contains secret information about hidden treasure? A map perhaps?

Bonus Idea ★

The caretaker has dug up a small chest in the school grounds and has handed it over to Year 6 as he thought they might be interested.

After one such event, quotes from the children included:

- 'I enjoyed going out to look at the debris. It all looked real.'
- 'Parts of the spaceship were glowing and I thought it was made up , but me and my friends were talking about it at playtime, and now we're not sure.'
- 'The best bit was pretending to be reporters at the scene, and getting quotes from people to put into our newspaper reports.'
- 'I liked making up funny headlines for my newspaper'

Idea 3 Engineer an experience in which children discover interesting artefacts while, for example, digging to build a new path or garden in school. In advance, bury Greek remains, dinosaur bones or relics from World War II! This is a chance for the class to do their own research and reports, as well some creative writing on, for example, imagining the surrounding area has been bombed during an air raid.

Idea 4 A clutch of dragon's eggs appears in the playground. Children across Key Stage 2 become dragonologists and write a set of instructions on how to take care of the eggs, a report for the local newspaper about the unusual events, and a missing egg poster when one mysteriously disappeared.

Developing emotionally intelligent boys

Part 2

Emotional intelligence: Self-awareness

"It is vitally important that we help all our children to communicate their feelings by giving them the words they need."

Quite often boys are not as capable as girls of talking about and reflecting on their feelings.

As we know, sometimes children can significantly underestimate their ability and their performance. Sometimes they may overestimate. In my experience, some boys can regularly fall into the latter category.

A simple poster, like the one below, is a good way of encouraging pupils to rate their attitude to work and behaviour towards each other at the end of a day. The results can lead to some interesting and useful discussions.

Gold

I've been respectful.
I've worked really hard.
I've produced some brilliant work.
I've helped others out if they needed help.

Silver

I've been respectful.
I've worked as hard as I can.
I've produced some good work.

Bronze

I've only worked when I've been reminded.
I've produced some OK work.

Yellow

I've not been working.

White

I've been bothering others.

Self-esteem and aspirations

"80% of that boy's self-esteem is in your face – the smiles, the nods, the eye contact and so on. You can't do what I do every day, stand in front of large groups of people, unless you are getting the smiles and the nods and the eye contact, that's where you build confidence and self-esteem."

Boys do want to be successful, despite the way it may sometimes appear.

When you ask them, there's hardly one that doesn't want to drive a Ferrari or be a Premiership football player. (With regard to the latter you may like to point out that each large town and city in the UK produces one professional football player a year. Have wild and wonderful dreams, yes, but also have a plan B.) However, so often a lack of self-esteem kills even the most modest of aspirations. What is more, if they are struggling with work they will very often throw up a smokescreen by misbehaving. Why? Because they would far rather be seen to be not bothered about winning, than to be trying and not winning. It may not always feel like a cry for help, but it very often it is. Here are some points to consider.

Teaching Tip

Get all pupils to submit an entry to a 'My Dream' competition, saying what it is they dream of becoming and why. Professionally photograph the winners dressed as judges, footballers, architects, policemen, whatever their dreams were, and display them prominently.

- Remember from your training that for every negative comment you deliver, children need at least three positive comments. A recent report suggested that that ratio needs to be closer to eight to one!
- They need to have self-belief, of course, but they also need to know that *you* believe in them.
- Praise must never be phony. Boys will be onto you; they know phony when they hear it.
- Ask your TA or manager to take an inventory of praise and criticism, by gender.

Give responsibility and raise self-esteem

"Teaching someone else what you've just been taught yourself is the most effective way of learning."

Giving boys responsibility is an important way to develop their self-esteem and confidence.

Boys can be put in charge of the library; they can be asked to help younger children with reading or with playground play; they can become a member of the school council or eco team.

At one primary school in Bradford, the pupils have their own office. Every visitor has to make an appointment (even the head teacher!). The visitor is met by a pupil, who proudly shows them round and explains the duty rotas of the various teams operating in and out of the office. Inside the office, there are spaces dedicated to the school bank, the health and safety team, the school eco team, the community team, and the peer mediator and buddy team. There is conference seating for the school council and a general working area where pupils work on a particular theme at lunchtimes: for example, one week it was an environmental theme, and posters and models were created by anyone who cared to join in. Members of the various teams complete a personal development survey on a regular basis. The impact on self-esteem and confidence is astounding!

Asking boys to take the role of 'expert' in class sessions is also a great way to boost their self-esteem and confidence. Many boys love to stand up and tell everyone everything they know about something.

Building self-confidence one day at a time

"This experience taught me that children's individual needs often require a very individual approach."

By using very simple tools we can change a child's view of themselves in a very powerful way.

This story from Reception teacher Zoe Wilson is a powerful example of using simple tools to maximum effect.

"Amongst my key children was a boy who had never spoken at nursery. The day I started I met his mother who, I had been informed, refused to believe this. I shared my concern that her son didn't speak or interact with anyone, but I stressed that some children take a long time to settle into a new environment. She seemed relieved and I promised I would try and address the situation.

The school SENCO recommended I tried praising him for any small utterance. I began by saying 'hello' and as soon as he replied I gave him a big white sticker that said 'today I talked to...' For the first couple of weeks, my name was the only name on the sticker, but by the end of week four he had at least four or five staff names on his sticker every day.

He became much more confident in the classroom, evident to the other children who began initiating conversation with him, something which had never happened before. Right up until the end of summer term he continued talking at nursery, and was even witnessed shouting!"

Teaching Tip

If a child has done something well, write it on an address label that they wear all day (e.g. 'David has done a great piece of drama today'). Any adult that meets David needs to compliment David. If they have time to chat about it they can do so. They then wear the sticker home, which means that they have something positive to talk about the minute they get there.

Self-esteem wordle

"David is just awesome at drama."

Building self-esteem with a wordle is simple, visually effective and fun.

By way of enabling the new teacher to learn all about their new class, group your class in small groups of friends and ask each group to do the following.

- Write down a list of all the positive characteristics of their friends, taking each one in turn. They need around a dozen or more.
- Give them a list to start the ball rolling: very funny, brilliant at drama, a whizz at spelling, a genius with story ideas, amazing at maths, a fantastic reader, a kind friend, a helpful friend.
- Now ask them to rank each person's list in turn.
- They should then enter their lists onto the wordle page as follows. If 'awesome at drama' comes first, with twelve points, then type this in twelve times. If clever at maths is only mentioned once then this only needs to be added once.
- Press the button and let wordle do the magic.
- Over the course of a few days use the wordles as the basis of a one-to-one chat. Ascertain if they are happy with the descriptions, etc.

Organising the class in groups of friends is very often a boy's preferred way of working. Boys often say to me that if they get sat next to somebody that they don't get on with and they get stuck, they'll stay stuck.

Become totally incompetent: Raise self-esteem

"You're going to learn this today, boys, but I'm not going to teach you." Paul Ginnis.

Boys love a challenge. Use this fact to engage them in a lesson from the outset.

Don't boys just love it when you make a mistake on the smart board? My advice: make more mistakes. Become totally incompetent. Try some of the following ideas and comments.

- 'I'm not sure I can remember how far we got last time with this.'
- Pretend that you have things to prepare before the lesson begins, and ask a member of the class to take over delivering the opening to a lesson by reminding the class what happened last time.
- 'You're going to learn all about Victorian childhood today, but I'm not going to teach you!'
- Misspellings on the smartboard.
- Claim that there are certain words that you have problems with and you need someone to remind you whenever they pop up (choose words that the class frequently have problems with!).
- Hand out rewards for spotting deliberate mistakes when you are reading something out loud.
- Make deliberate errors in a new display.
- 'I give up, how are you going to remember this work for your test?'
- 'If you think you can do better, come up and have a go!' (In good humour, not anger!)
- It's been a long time since we read this book – I can't remember a single thing about it!

Taking it Further

Plan a session which allows the opportunity for them to take on board a challenge, such as 'Oh no, I've lost the instructions for how to make a battery tester', which will almost invariably result in a boy saying, 'I'll do that for you, I'll sort it!'

What a juicy mistake

"The fear of failure has a significant impact on their attitude to work."

Put a positive spin on mistakes.

When they make mistakes, boys often feel that they are just a failure and their response is to say that they can't do it or they are hopeless at a particular task. Teachers can sometimes reinforce these negative feelings when we find it hard to disguise our own disappointment.

Of course, as adults, we know that making mistakes is how we learn. In business and industry they love mistakes. There are loads of examples. For instance, WD40 (that we use to get cars started) is so named because the first 39 attempts at making it didn't work. Seven Up? They tried to launch six times unsuccessfully!

Why not celebrate their mistakes?

Encourage a positive attitude in your school by:

- Looking out for 'juicy mistakes' and responding positively: 'Well Michael, that was a really juicy mistake – let's think of all the things we can learn from that!'
- Encouraging other children in the class to come up with ideas around the mistake.
- Displaying the mistake on the 'Juicy Mistakes' board.
- Creating a map alongside the mistake to demonstrate all the learning that has come from it.

Praise

"Boys need praise, praise and more praise."

"The praise we give needs to be specific and never phoney"

Discuss with your colleagues how praise is used. Encourage them to:

- give specific, rather than generic, praise
- praise the action and behaviour, rather than the person.

If you say 'David, you're brilliant', David has no idea why you have said he is brilliant. Therefore the chance of him repeating whatever it was is very low.

Saying, 'David, I love the way you have started your story with a wonderful description of the setting you've used. Some of the words that you have chosen are perfect!' will help him to recognise what it is he has done to earn the praise, rather than simply saying, 'What a great writer you are!'.

And the praise should never be phoney. David hasn't put his hand up for ages, but today he has. 'David that was a stunning response!' but David knows it wasn't a stunning response and he won't be putting his hand up again for some time.

Teaching Tip

Remember that when/if you feel the need to make a negative comment, they need at least three positives in order to maintain their self-esteem and confidence. Recent research suggests eight positives to one negative.

Taking it Further

Ask your in-class support to monitor for a day (without telling you which day!) the number of positive and negative comments you make.

Use text messages home as part of your reward system. 'Your Errol has done a fantastic piece of work in literacy today!' See Idea 47.

Praise postcards

"For some children, this may be the first time good news has travelled home."

There are many praise postcards commercially available, but homemade ones are best. Praise postcards are widely used now in primary and secondary schools, not least because the biggest miscreant will have a praise postcard stuck to the fridge until they retire. For some it's the first time good news has travelled home and for those worried about being made fun of by their peers it's an opportunity to celebrate away from their prying eyes.

What is already a great idea can be improved by the following tweaks.

- Ensure that postcards arrive home on a Saturday so that the whole family can celebrate them together.
- Make your own high-quality praise postcards with blank space for comments rather than the templates that are found on commercially available ones.
- Don't limit praise postcards to academic achievement. Also celebrate being helpful, being kind to a friend, being thoughtful, being punctual, producing great homework.
- Use the opportunity to give specific guidance on the cards to help parents. For example, at Armitage C of E Primary School in Manchester they produce their own beautiful, professional-standard homemade cards showing pictures of some of their children reading. In bold letters on the front are comments like 'I like reading because my mummy and daddy say well done and that makes me happy.' Or 'I like reading at school and my dad reads me stories at bedtime and that gets me to sleep.' or 'I always listen really well when I am being read to at school. I like being read to at home as well because my mummy does funny voices.'

Dealing with feelings

"It's easier to build strong boys than to mend broken men."

The work that we do in schools to help develop emotional intelligence is vitally important for all pupils. What is particularly important as far as boys are concerned is that we give them the words to unclench their hearts.

When children phone Childline, it would appear that girls tend to phone when the severity of their problem is at a significantly earlier stage than boys. It often takes boys much longer to open up, but when they do they're alright. This illustrates just why the work on emotional intelligence in schools is so important.

The differences in the speed of language development between most boys and girls is widely understood. What is also true is that girls are far more capable of talking about their feelings, as they spend more time doing just that. Boys often have problems when called upon to reflect upon and express their feelings.

Discuss with colleagues ways in which you can help boys to articulate their feelings. For example:

- be aware that a change in mood may be a cry for help
- 'check in' from time to time, by asking in an informal way how boys are feeling
- give names to the emotions they appear to be feeling or are demonstrating.

Teaching Tip

Use examples from stories of how men and boys have dealt with feelings, or use role play to explore dilemmas and problems, and help boys to work through emotions.

Taking it Further

Give boys practical exercises to help with feelings or stress, anxiety or anger (see the relaxation techniques in Idea 41).

In the right state

"Only happy and calm children learn."

We need to be constantly aware of how the children in our care are feeling. How often do we ask 'How do you feel today?'

In Limeside primary school in Oldham, whilst being shown the school by the head teacher, I became steadily aware that she was taking note of a rather unusual display on every classroom door.

There on every single one, about four feet from the floor, was a thumbs up sign and the words 'Feeling good today!', then a space. A foot lower down was a sign showing a level hand, with the thumb tucked away with 'I'm feeling OK today' written next to it, then a space. A foot below that was a thumbs down sign next to which it said 'I'm not very happy today', with another space underneath.

The spaces below each sign were there for the children to stick the laminated picture of their own face (about the size of a matchbox) as they clocked in to school that day.

At one door we both smiled to see one boy's picture, about two feet above the thumbs up sign, almost on the ceiling. He would have to have jumped some distance in the air to stick on his picture. Somebody was going to have a great day! Outside another classroom, however, there were four or five faces under the thumbs down sign. 'Oh dear, I shall be calling in there later,' The headteacher remarked.

Feeling good, working well

"How do I get them in the right state for learning?"

Simple relaxation techniques can really help.

Happy, calm children learn well, but nurturing this ideal state can be a challenge, especially after a '*boy*sterous' playtime! Teaching simple relaxation techniques to children will help them to:

- increase mental alertness and focus
- control impulsive behaviour
- work more efficiently.

YogaBugs is an organisation that provides training in the use of yoga in schools. I first saw yoga in action in a primary school in a rough, tough rugby playing area in Yorkshire. I watched, amazed, as every half hour a new group would charge into the hall, then quickly lie down on yoga mats as the yoga teacher gently intoned her directions, accompanied by gentle music and the aroma of mandarin oil (the only oil that no one is allergic to apparently!). Then each class in turn would calmly float out of the hall thirty minutes later.

Try the following simple exercises with your children.

Snake breath Breathe in through the nose to the count of five – hold to the count of five – breathe out for as long as you can make the breath last.

Power breath Stand with legs slightly apart, as if rooted to the ground – imagine a golden cord running up through the spine – place the hands, fingertips touching, on the tummy and breathe gently and fully in and out, feeling the fingers move apart and then back together again.

Peer massage

"Peer massage? I've seen it transform children, classes and whole schools."

Many teachers turn to yoga, meditation, mindfulness, massage and so on to help reduce tension and enhance their wellbeing. If it's good for you then have you thought that maybe it could be good for children too? After all, only happy and calm children learn.

Taking it Further

Search for information about training. You and your children will be glad you did! Training providers include:

- Child2Child
- The Massage in Schools Association
- The Peer Massage Project
- Relax Kids
- YogaBugs.

Many schools have found that peer massage programmes, used on a daily basis, are very helpful for children. There are many boys and girls who never experience positive touch in their homes and for them, above all, the benefits of peer massage can be immense. Peer massage programmes require training and full parental permission. so are not undertaken lightly, but the benefits can be substantial. Studies and observations have shown that peer massage can have many benefits. The effects are instant and can last a lifetime. Peer massage has a calming effect, significantly reduces bullying and aggression, and helps improve concentration, confidence and self-esteem. When practised every day for five minutes or so, it gets children in the right emotional state for learning.

There have been countless reports in recent years suggesting that our children at primary level are stressed. A UNICEF-sponsored report looking at childhood in 22 countries suggested that Britain's children were the unhappiest, with concerns about testing, transition, and homework. Positive touch can help make a difference. Child2Child trainer Susan Ainscough asks the children how they feel when they have been massaging each other. One six-year-old told her, 'It made me feel appreciated!'

7% is the words that we use

"If we have to shout we have already lost them."

Creating the right environment for learning is down to us, the professionals in the room. We need to create an atmosphere that is calm and conducive to learning

When we communicate, the words that we use are the least important elements of that communication (7% apparently!). The rest is in our tone of voice, our body language, our demeanour, whether we crouch down to communicate at a child's level or loom over them. If we have to shout at a class, very often it's too late, we've already lost them. If we are constantly having to raise our voice the atmosphere we create is not conducive to learning. Consider these questions:

- How many times do you have to raise your voice? How often is this to girls and how often to boys?
- How many times do you praise boys and girls? What is the nature of that praise?
- Is there a noticeable difference in the way in which your eye contact, demeanour, and tone of voice varies when you address boys and girls?
- Are you asking roughly equal numbers of boys and girls questions throughout the day?
- Is there a marked difference between the type of questions you ask girls and boys?

All in all, do you think you talk to boys and girls differently? Boys tell me that teachers definitely do, and, what's more, it makes them feel that teachers prefer girls! And they have offered me that as one of the reasons why boys don't do as well as girls in school.

> **Teaching Tip**
>
> Hold a discussion around girls and boys and their behaviour and the responses of teachers. Or, if you're feeling brave, ask them to produce a piece of role play.

Developing emotionally intelligent classrooms

"They don't shout at girls because they don't want to make them cry."

Do you think you talk to boys and girls differently? You probably do!

Since the early nineties, I have had hundreds of discussions with groups of boys about why they are not doing as well as girls. One thing that always comes up is that they believe that teachers prefer girls just because of the way we talk to them! 'You can tell,' one boy told me. 'How?' I asked. 'They don't shout at girls because they don't want to make them cry. But they shout at us.' 'Why?' 'Because they think we're stronger.'

A parent told me that at the end of her first week in nursery her daughter could recite the full names of all the boys but only the first names of the girls. In a similar vein, a friend told me that after her daughter's first day in nursery she came home and said 'There are two Neils in nursery, Mummy – and one's called Neil Behave!'

One teacher told me she discovered she didn't ask a single open-ended question to a boy all day. She was so used to girls being more reflective that she just asked the boys quick yes/no questions. Another discovered that she hadn't asked a single girl a maths question all morning.

It's always an interesting exercise to ask someone to observe the frequency, the nature and the quality of the interactions you have with boys and girls. Try it!

Don't say a word!

"Silence is golden"

Sometimes the most effective ways of improving behaviour are simple, non-verbal cues.

Bill Rogers, an expert in classroom behaviour, suggests that even for the very youngest in our care, we can actually affect behaviour in a positive way without saying a word. Try these non-verbal cues.

Teaching Tip

Introduce the six non-verbal cues as an experiment for a week and then ask the class if they approve.

- Cross your index finger, then beckon with your right hand to indicate 'cross your legs and face the front'.
- Raise one hand and cover your mouth with the other to indicate 'hands up without calling out'.
- Put one hand over the other and pull it into your chest to indicate 'keep hands and feet to yourself'.
- Touch one eye, then one ear, with a forefinger, and use a beckoning hand to the front of the room to indicate 'eyes and ears this way now'.
- Holds up a thumb and forefinger a little distance apart to indicate 'use your partner voice'. This is an effective reminder during on-task learning time as the teacher is moving around the room.
- Use thumb and two fingers, rotating an imaginary volume control, to indicate 'quiet down'.

Classroom Behaviour, B. Rogers, SAGE Publications.

The good news board

"The headteacher told me you've been very helpful this morning. Well done, I'm proud of you."

Here is a tried and tested strategy that helps to change boys' attitudes towards themselves. It gives them the message that teachers are noticing them for all the right reasons!

Teaching Tip

When you have created a good news notice board, monitor it on a regular basis for any changes in attitude, behaviour and performance.

Identify individuals who are a cause of particular concern, starting with those who I call the peer police cadets: the ones at the top end of school who are dragging other boys down. Display photos of them on a notice board in the staffroom, and invite staff to add 'good news' sticky notes. Reinforce that there should never be anything negative, just good news. This gives everyone in the school the chance to share evidence of positive behaviour, and to reinforce it with the child, 'Miss McRae told me you were very understanding when someone hurt themselves in the playground this lunchtime – well done!'

In my experience promoting this in countless schools, the first time one of these boys gets a piece of good news from the notice board, the rest of the boys will suddenly become desperate for a piece of good news themselves.

It changes a lot of boys' attitudes towards themselves. It changes a lot of teachers' attitudes towards those boys, too, and most significantly the attitudes of teachers who have never even taught the boys, just heard them talked about in the staffroom!

Celebrate!

"Your Marcus has done a great piece of work in literacy this morning."

As they get older, a lot of boys shy away from publicly celebrating success as a result of peer pressure. Dealing with peer pressure is, of course, of fundamental importance, but so too is thinking of ways that boys can receive the praise that they deserve.

Celebrating boys' successes within the school community and with parents can help in many ways.

Send texts to parents telling them that their child has done a particularly good piece of work, or has been helpful or kind. 'Your Edward has just done a great piece of work in literacy this morning!' 'Great, Marcus's mum is on her way to the shops so she's going to buy him a little treat.' Most importantly, they've got something positive to talk about the moment he gets home.

Many schools who have tried this have said that parents often respond to the school and that sometimes it has contributed significantly to the home-school partnership. In other words, it has literally started a dialogue between home and school that previously never existed.

Also see praise postcards in Idea 38.

Teaching Tip

Ask boys what kinds of rewards suit them best and how they'd like to be rewarded. Where? By whom? Is there a growing reluctance to celebrate their achievements publicly by Year 6? If so, then clearly action is required.

Teaching and learning

Part 3

Pushing all the right buttons

"Boys love a challenge. Give them a challenge the minute they set foot in the door."

Assessment for Learning in general, and success criteria in particular, could have been created with just boys in mind.

Teaching Tip

In Key Stage 1 and 2, children could have their own challenge books in which they would can record the challenges they complete each week. The teacher sets the challenges and the children complete them in their own time.

The use of success criteria is a powerful tool in helping boys achieve; its systematic nature has a strong appeal for boys, and the element of challenge that it presents is also compelling.

- Present the aims of the lesson as a 'challenge' on the board, listing success criteria as a series of targets.
- Allow children to select their own success criteria from the list.
- Allow children to choose their own way of presenting the information, therefore encouraging them to work to their own strengths, as well as taking the lead in their own learning. Similarly, the Suffolk report on boys and writing suggests that, by giving boys a choice after a particular activity or discussion between writing a short report, a poem, a flowchart, a newspaper article or a mindmap etc, will improve their motivation and improve the quality of work.
- Asking boys to read through their work for mistakes can be a fruitless exercise, but getting them to look through someone else's work for mistakes? They love that challenge!
- Encourage children to give themselves scores for motivation, achieving the success criteria, and the quality of their work.

Switch on!

"If I hadn't seen that piece of work I wouldn't know what a level six looked like!"

Boys need to see the big picture as it helps them connect with their learning.

Boys are more likely to engage with the lesson if they can see the sense and purpose of what they are doing and where it fits in the larger scheme of things. Display an enlarged planning map of the topic on a classroom wall and refer to this frequently during each session, or use the interactive whiteboard.

- At the end of each session, invite children to write 'I'm not clear on this bit' sticky notes, and keep these for the next session.
- Review the last session's work at the beginning of each session and respond to the issues raised by the sticky notes.
- Ask children to produce their own mind map or graphic organiser for the topic – this will help them to make connections that are meaningful for them in their learning. Graphic organisers of any kind can be very useful for most boys, as around about the age of four or five they tend to develop a right hemisphere dominance; which means they want, and indeed need, to know the big picture.
- Boys also need to know what a good piece of work looks like. Display work from previous pupils (with names removed) who have achieved a range of levels.

Teaching Tip

For younger children, introduce a learning wall (as a classroom display or on an interactive white board) divided into three sections: what we already know, what we want to find out, and what we have learned. Add samples of their work to the wall.

Switch on! Challenge!

"Boys don't all love competition. Boys who win competitions love them; those who rarely or never do hate them; they become crushing experiences. However, virtually all boys love a challenge."

Boys respond very positively to a challenge, so ask your staff to consider the following.

Teaching Tip

Based on this list, create your own content for quick challenges that are relevant to your current area of work.

- When does the first challenge appear in your lesson plan? Research suggests that it's usually ten minutes before the first challenge appears. Up until then there is a lot of low level activity, settling in, recapping, getting organised.
- We know boys love a challenge; hit them with a quick challenge at the outset. Consider a quick piece of problem solving, or a ridiculous statement or question written up on the board.

Try some of the following quick ideas at the beginning of the session.

- **In common** Encourage them to make unlikely connections, for example, 'What do books and teeth have in common?'
- **The combo** Connect the topic to another topic, such as 'List what's good about a toyshop. Can you use your ideas to improve the design of the library?'
- **The question is...**Give them the answer, and ask for five questions.
- **Ridiculous ideas** Ask a crazy question, for example, 'What would happen if teapots were made out of chocolate?'
- **What if?** Ask a hypothetical question, 'What if there was no such thing as school?'
- **Different uses** Come up with different uses for something, for example, 'How many uses can you can think of for a ruler?'
- **The invention** Invent something, for example, 'Think of a really clever way of remembering what you've just been taught.'

Taking it Further

Challenge them to be creative in their approach. Encourage them to select success criteria from your list and to think of the most original and creative way possible to meet it.

Come along, it's your time you're wasting

"The most used piece of equipment in my classroom is a stopwatch."

It's all about timing! Presenting boys with a time limit can provide them with the kind of challenge that really appeals.

Teachers often say that the most used piece of equipment in their classroom is a stopwatch or sand timer, or a Countdown clock! In an activity like Philosophy for Children (see Idea 77) the time limit element is clearly part of the attraction. Similarly, a time limit is one of the key elements that increases the likelihood of success for boys when they are engaged in a group task. Group work works best for boys when there is appropriate grouping, where they are given a clear role and a real sense of purpose, where there is a clear outcome, and when there is a time limit that gives that element of challenge.

On the other hand, sometimes boys say they get frustrated if they are not allowed to finish something before moving on. Ever heard – 'I'm taking my time with this because I like it!'? Sometimes we need to:

- be flexible with time limits
- in Early Years, leave resources out longer (sometimes children get frustrated if something is tidied away and they were still interacting with it or even just thinking about it)
- be aware when boys start to show the first signs of frustration when they want to finish a piece of work before moving on to the next, and act accordingly.

Teaching Tip

In Early Years it is common practice to use a piece of music for tidying up (Mission Impossible is popular). Often, though, boys will lose interest midway through, disappear on to the mat and start spinning on their bums!

Change the rules. Say 'Let's tidy up now until the music finishes. Then freeze in whatever position you are in!' They'll carry on until you signal, because they love musical statues!

Connect to their emotions

If boys don't see the sense and purpose in doing something they simply won't engage with it. Connecting their learning is particularly important for boys, and if that connection is made to their emotions it becomes very powerful.

When we invite boys to suspend their disbelief, some kind of 'wow' factor can be irresistible.

The most effective way of connecting learning is by connecting to emotions. This account from an adult visitor to a lesson demonstrates this:

"We were handed torches, and asked to wait outside the classroom. Anticipation quickly grew. When we entered the room, it was in darkness and the furniture had been moved. The teacher invited us to use our torches to explore the various Victorian artefacts, newspaper cuttings and photographs scattered around the floor. Silence prevailed, there were no collisions, and the concentration level was high. After some time, the lights were switched on and we were asked to select one item.

I chose a newspaper headline about a mill accident in which a girl had been injured. The boy next to me chose a photograph of smartly dressed boys sat in rows in a schoolroom. We were asked to explain our interest in our item: for me, it was my experience of visiting my father at work in a mill when I was a child, and remembering the deafening noise and the frightening machines. The next stage was to work with a partner and decide how we could create a piece of work by connecting our items with the person beside us. My partner suggested a piece of drama showing the contrast between the boys' lives, and the girl's. The teacher developed weeks of work based on this experience."

Activate the learning

"Teaching and learning styles are not rocket science."

Boy-friendly chunks are best, and this includes short-term targets, short-term goals and short-term rewards.

The vast majority of boys tend to prefer learning in more active ways all the way through school. It will come as no surprise when I say that whenever I ask boys in high schools what their favourite subjects are, nine times out of ten they will choose the most active subjects, and then after that they'll just work hard for the teachers that they like. The vast majority of teachers tend to be visual learners, as are most adults. We tend to teach in the way in which we learn best, therefore there is the potential for a mismatch in teaching and learning styles that we need to address.

This does not mean that we suddenly need to start teaching them all in an active way all the time. Apart from anything else, we'd be dead on our feet by Wednesday lunchtime! We would also be doing them a disservice because, although we do need to work to their strengths, we also need to develop their areas of weakness so they become well-rounded learners. But it does mean that we need to ask ourselves, 'Are we providing enough active learning elements in our session, in our morning, in our day, to ensure that boys do engage with their learning and are motivated and energised enough to learn?'

A preferred learning style is the most powerful tool in their kit when they are struggling with something new, and preparing for tests and exams.

Teaching Tip

Ensure that an appropriate amount of time in the day is available for active learning. Place a particular priority on active learning when boys are learning something new and when they are preparing for tests. Instigate 'brain breaks': short periods of rest from their ongoing work or quick bursts of physical activity to re-energise and refocus boys and to ensure that lessons are delivered in 'boy-friendly chunks'.

Aw...do we have to write about it, Miss?

"There's always a catch!"

Making a record is an important way to consolidate learning and 'show what you know', but the record does not always have to be in writing.

You may have noticed how, on a bad day, some boys start to lose interest towards the end of a lesson, as they know there is a catch coming! A teacher told me of a boy who was glum faced on the coach on the way back from a theatre trip. She asked him if he had enjoyed the play. He replied that yes, he had, but he just realised he's going to have to write about it!

Here are some simple ideas to try in your school.

- Use piggy-back learning. This is where two able pupils are trained to teach two other pupils, who then pass their knowledge on until everyone 'gets it'. This strategy works well for many subjects and also develops speaking and listening skills.
- Give children a choice of format for presenting their work, e.g. a mind map, a flowchart, a bubble map etc. This allows them to take the lead in their own learning, and to work to their strengths.
- For younger children, recording their responses on a recording microphone/device can be effective.
- In Early Years use talking tins (a good use for these is for the children to record commentary about what's going on in the picture of them playing and learning), talking postcards and talking books.

Stop mental truancy!

"Trying to learn without reviewing and reflecting is like trying to fill the bath without putting the plug in." Mike Hughes, Education consultant and author of *Tweak to Transform*.

For many boys the weakest link in their learning process is their inability to reflect. If in doubt, check their written evaluations!

Opportunities to reflect throughout the lesson together provide a vital tool for developing learning. Yet it is tempting, at the end of the lesson, to ask a question and look for the answer as quickly as possible. Often, the same hands are raised, and the answer is supplied so quickly that many children have not been given enough time to engage in the process of reflection. We also might find a group of boys who simply aren't listening, they're just playing mental truancy. Here are some different approaches.

- Give children 'thinking time' or 'day-dreaming time' before eliciting a response.
- Pair/share – ask children to discuss the question for two minutes, and then randomly choose a pair to respond.
- 'I wonder?' – instead of asking a direct question, say, for example, 'I wonder how John did that so well?' This is an effective strategy when working with Early Years children, or children who are reluctant to communicate.
- Have a 'Wonderwall', where you record children's best questions.
- Play the devil's advocate – 'Can we imagine someone else having a different point of view?'
- Encourage the children to ask questions of each other!

Teaching Tip

At the end of the day ask, at random, 'What was the best question you asked today?'

Taking it Further

Assign one child in a group to take photographs of, or film, a group activity. Encourage the group to describe what they were learning.

Use Philosophy for Education approaches www.sapere.org.uk to develop powerful questioning skills.

Play

Part 4

But they don't know how to play!

"We have an inborn drive to learn. It's called play."

Anthropologists working all over the world in a vast range of cultures report that all children play from dawn 'till dusk. However, there has been a serious reduction in play in the last decade and a serious increase in depression and anxiety amongst young people.

The sad fact is that many of us, adults and children alike, have forgotten how to play. Ben Kingston-Hughes, a trainer in children's play, works with parents, lunchtime supervisors, teachers and children, and reports that sometimes 'parents become quite tearful because they don't know how to play.' After training they are encouraged to provide more positive play experiences for their children outside the school. The benefits to many boys who are taught how to play include a reduction in aggressive behaviour, fewer lunchtime incidents, an increase in self-esteem and communication skills, and more. Perhaps above all, they are in a better frame of mind for learning in the afternoon.

- Consider training for lunchtime supervisors, staff and parents.
- Organise for Year 6 boys to teach boys in the younger years games for the playground or indoors.
- Produce leaflets to send home to explain the rules for outdoor and indoor games.
- Get pupils to interview grandparents about childhood games they played with friends at home and at school and then get the pupils to teach the class.

Play more, learn more

"Take care, free range children" – Sign seen outside a country primary school.

Whilst more play would be beneficial to everybody, there are particular benefits for boys here.

Many feel that the push in education is for more schooling and less playing, but it is worth remembering that in those areas of Scandinavia where boys are doing just as well as girls, it is widely agreed that the main reason is that children don't start school formally until they are seven, and prior to that they are learning actively, outside, and largely through play. Many of the areas within the Social and Emotional Aspects of Development and the Social and Emotional Aspects of Learning work in schools, such as developing empathy and self control, can be covered through the imaginative use of play.

Survey the kind of play that goes on in the playground for a week. Notice the most commonly played games and how much imaginative play there is on display. Is the experience of many at lunchtime being told what they have to do for forty-five minutes?

Discuss as a staff how you might create more opportunities for imaginative play by using, for example:

- a stage platform in the playground
- a storytelling chair
- pop-up tents and den-making material
- wild areas for exploration
- a designated hut containing materials for role play (see Idea 12).

More and more schools are presenting role play opportunities at lunchtimes and noting that boys are in a far better frame of mind for learning in the afternoon.

> **Teaching Tip**
>
> Board games, either indoors or large scale outdoor games, can help develop many of the qualities described here. Many schools tell me that chess is a very significant activity for many boys – why not create a large scale playground version?

Parents need to know this stuff

Part 5

Parents need to know this stuff 1

"If we don't get these messages across to parents it's like writing on that little internal whiteboard and every night they're going home and it's being wiped clean."

Try this tried and tested approach to delivering a parent's workshop that will inform and engage them in discovering what they can do to help their boys succeed.

Year after year, the headlines at exam time shout about girls outperforming boys. Yet there is very little calm debate about the truth of this or any explanation for parents as to why it might be happening. Holding a workshop for parents that looks at boys' achievement can help to address their concerns and give them valuable advice and ideas about how they can help. Wherever possible, try to encourage dads – or other males from the close and extended family – to attend.

From the experience of delivering hundreds of parents' sessions, the most common comment is 'It was great, but the parents we want to see are the ones that never come.' It is always thus. But some schools manage it. See the Teaching Tip, and Idea 60, for some advice.

Give parents a balanced overview of the situation, including:

- the statistics concerning boys' and girls' performance nationally and internationally
- the levels of performance within your school
- a range of reasons as to why boys may underachieve, e.g. lack of independence when they start school, the fact that boys and girls develop fine motor skills at different rates, the fact that girls tend to use more language in their play from an early age, and often have a more positive attitude towards reading.

Parents need to know this stuff 2

"This work is not to the detriment of girls, it is for the benefit of everybody."

Continue the meeting started in Idea 58 by explaining in general terms what your school is doing to address the issue of boys' achievement

The first thing you could mention is that you have put boys on your school agenda! And, most importantly, explain that this focus on boys will not be detrimental to girls. As I have always said, anything we do that looks at the attitude, the behaviour and motivation of boys will have a knock-on effect on girls, especially because it can sometimes be a small group of boy that behave in ways that are detrimental to girls. Also, if through this work we help develop caring young men (as has always been my mission) then that surely is beneficial for girls too.

Talk about how parents can help:

- by encouraging boys to be more independent – dressing themselves, making lists of things they need for school, etc.
- ensuring that boys encounter positive male role models in the close and extended family
- becoming involved with the school (give examples of particular projects)
- developing literacy skills by reading and writing with their boys
- developing speaking and listening skills, by, for example, sitting round a table and eating and talking together.

Depending on the particular issues for boys in your school, you may wish to explore one or more topics in detail.

Teaching Tip

Present parents with some useful information and ideas on, for example, improving speaking and listening skills. If time allows, hold a discussion that will get parents thinking about how they interact with their boys at home and give them tips for improving the amount and quality of their interactions.

Parents need to know this stuff 3

"Yes, but the parents we need to see are the ones that never come."

There is always the problem of reaching the hard-to-reach parents. We must double, triple, quadruple our efforts.

Think positive! What you do have is a small group of enthusiastic parents, who could prove invaluable in reaching out to other parents.

In the final part of your parents' workshop, break into small groups (each group to include a member of staff) and allow five to ten minutes for a discussion on any ideas they may have on how to engage hard-to-reach parents.

Put together a leaflet of ideas, not from the school, or even the local authority, but from parents (with your blessing and editorial skills) to give to other parents.

You could also try the 'adopt a parent' challenge, with each parent bringing along another parent who didn't attend the last meeting!

Have a parents session at 2:30pm/3:30pm and then again at 7pm to suit everyone's best time and show that you have 100 percent expectation that all parents will come along.

Double up the meeting with another, for example, a pre-SATs meeting or Governors AGM.

Top tips for parents – Early Years 1

"If you stop answering questions, he'll stop asking them!"

Research shows that, for example, boys tend to use less language in their play. If we want to raise their achievement, it's important to get them speaking and listening right from the start.

You can help by:

- commenting on play and activity, i.e. showing an interest in what he is doing and asking questions about it
- talking with him, not at him
- being patient, listening with interest to what he has to say, handing conversation back to him, and not leaping in with an answer
- talking as you do jobs around the house
- pointing out things you see around you when you're out and about and chatting about them.
- discussing the films and programmes you watch together, e.g. what each of you liked about the programme, which characters were most interesting, which bits were funniest/cleverest
- playing a game together with any related character toys and games
- encouraging him to ask questions by always answering them.

Teaching Tip

Use the information here as a starting point to help you produce an information leaflet or display for parents.

Taking it Further

For a more hard hitting and fun approach, produce a 'Talking in the Early Years' DVD, with you and individual children, or parent volunteers.

Bonus Idea

Make a public appeal to all parents asking them not to be on their mobile phones when they pick up their child. Tell them that their child may be desperate to tell them all about something they've done today!

Top tips for parents – Early Years 2

"Even little changes can make a big difference!"

We need to show how parents can help at home in the Early Years.

Parents can help by:

- encouraging boys to be more independent, e.g. dressing themselves/making lists of things they need for school
- encouraging boys to talk about how they are feeling
- praising boys, whether for academic performance or for good behaviour
- reading with boys (both males and females in the family need to do this, and don't stop reading to children or with him because he can read)
- helping boys to develop speaking and listening skills
- talking about reading
- making some time to read stories together (even five minutes a day is a good start); read with as much expression as possible, bring the characters to life.
- talking about the pictures, drawing attention to details, e.g. 'how do you think he or she is feeling?', 'what is happening behind him/her?'
- encouraging boys to predict what is going to happen next in the story
- asking boys to retell the story – either to you or to another member of the family.
- helping your child's reading with essential tips, fun activities and free eBooks (see www.oxfordowl.co.uk).

Developing independence

"But he's got legs!"

It is important that we get the message home about independence before children start school. Parents need to know there is a very strong correlation between a child being independent when they start school and becoming an independent learner.

In conversations with Early Years practitioners they often refer to parents' perceptions of their boys' levels of competence being completely at odds with their perception. For example, often they will carry their little son in from the car and hand him over in mid air. The practitioner feels like saying 'But he's got legs!'

Or the parent, on arrival at nursery at the end of the day, gives the young one a dummy and/or straps them immediately into their pushchair. Or the parent arrives with a bottle complete with teat when he's been drinking from a cup all day! Or the parent fails to praise the little one for a picture that the teacher has praised them to the hilt about. Early Years practitioners recall parents saying 'He's too young to do that!' when he's perfectly capable of doing it in nursery. One teacher related how she gets one boy to put on his shoes and fasten them five minutes before their parent arrives. If she doesn't then they will immediately do it for him, even though he is perfectly capable.

It may sometimes be very difficult to communicate these messages to parents face to face, but try the tips in the next idea.

Teaching Tip

Create a series of stickers that proudly announce 'I can fasten my own shoelaces', 'I can fasten my own coat', etc.

Taking it Further

Write a specific achievement on an address label and encourage any adult to praise them for it, e.g. I did a really good picture of a dinosaur today.

Taking the pressure off

"You told me that parental anxiety is catching and advised me to 'take my foot off the pedal'. I did, and the change in his attitude was wonderful to see."

Parents really need to know before their boy starts in Early Years that if they are anxious about his rate of development in reading or writing that anxiety is often communicated to him and it becomes detrimental to his development.

Taking it Further

At a pre-school meeting, give parents examples of how they can help develop fine motor skills effectively at home, e.g. by showing them 'Dough Disco' on You Tube.

Show them how they can help to develop a love of story, e.g. by showing them how you bring stories alive!

It doesn't matter if he can't write yet.

But it would help if he has well-developed fine motor skills.

It doesn't matter if he can't write his name yet.

But it would help if he recognised his name.

It doesn't matter if he can't read books yet.

But it would help if he were read to. If he was excited by stories, he could retell stories and join in with chants from familiar stories.

It doesn't matter if he can't draw a recognisable picture yet.

But it would help if he used materials to draw circles and lines.

It doesn't matter if he can't recognise letters of the alphabet yet.

But it would help if he could hear the initial letter sound in words.

Top tips for parents 1

"Readers will be leaders. Boys need to read, read, read"

Here is the kind of material you might use for a parents' session or information leaflet that will be useful at any age.

Many boys tend to switch off from reading when they have mastered the basics of *how* to read.

Enrol your son in your local library and, as much as possible, allow him to choose the books he wants to read for pleasure so that he doesn't seeing reading as an imposition. He may choose the same kind of book over and over, and go for books that appeal to his sense of mischief, are sometimes gross, or have humour that's quite edgy. He will move on eventually...when his teacher engages them with more substantial books, when his friends move on, or with *gentle* persuasion and encouragement on your part.

Sometimes a boy may choose books that are very easy. If this happens, he may be feeling a little unsure of his ability and he may be looking for reassurance. This will pass provided he doesn't feel pressurised.

When reading with your son, try to read with expression. Talk about the characters, plot and pictures along the way. Ask them to guess what might happen next, etc.

Give your son the opportunity to share the reading with you sometimes so he only has to do half of the work. Listening to you reading well will encourage him to do the same.

Make sure your son sees adults reading, particularly older males in the close and extended family.

Reading isn't just about books! Encourage your child to read when you are out and about together: labels, signs, posters, instructions... the list is endless. Words are everywhere – share them together!

Teaching Tip

Use these as a starting point for a parents' session then run a parents' workshop encompassing a range of issues around boys' achievement.

Taking it Further

Supply parents with a leaflet explaining the importance of reading, recommended books information about joining a library and so on.

Top tips for parents 2

"Catch them doing something well and praise them for it."

Accentuate the positive by ensuring that your positive comments outnumber the negatives by at least 3 to 1. This advice is useful at any age.

Teaching Tip

Use any or all of these as starting points in the parents' workshop.

It's important to reinforce that mistakes don't equal failure; it's the way we learn. Try this to illustrate your point.

Michael Jordan, one of the great American basketball players was dropped from his high school basketball team. A couple of years ago he wrote in a newspaper: 'I have missed more than 9000 shots in my career. I have lost almost 300 games. On 26 occasions I have been entrusted to take the game winning shot and I missed. I have failed over and over and over again in my life. And that is why I succeed, that is why I am a champion.'

Boys often feel that mistakes equal failure. Their response is to say that they can't do it. We have to catch them doing something well, give them lots of encouragement and make them feel they *can* do it.

All too often, boys see themselves as getting attention for all the wrong reasons; we need to give them lots of approval for all the right reasons! A good rule of thumb is to try to say three positive things to every negative. When giving praise, try to be specific about what it is your child has done. For example, say 'That is a great piece of writing. I like the way you've described the...' This way the child will be able to recognise what it is they have done to earn the praise.

If you have to say something negative, make it clear that it is the behaviour that you dislike and not the boy. Instead of 'How dare you be so rude!' say 'The way you said that was very rude!' Instead of 'You are horrible to your sister!' say, 'We all love you, Michael, but we don't like the way you treat your sister'.

Positive male
role models

Part 6

Positive male role models in the wider community

"Me and my granddad made this together."

There is an important role in the upbringing of boys for all older males in the close and extended family to play.

Taking it Further

Invite dads, granddads, uncles and older brothers to talk in the class about their occupation or profession.

If you ask boys who their male role models are – and I do this on a regular basis – they will frequently name sportsmen, and most commonly footballers. But the behaviour of some of these people is, all too often, far from exemplary, on or off the pitch. It is a problem that extends not just to football but even to the more 'gentlemanly' sports, where we can see yobbish and laddish behaviour. There are a few notable exceptions to this, but you can hardly blame children when, on being asked to name other role models, they come up with fictitious characters, e.g. Batman or Spiderman. Encouragingly, I also often hear children answer 'my dad', 'my granddad' or 'my brother'.

We know that need to raise awareness of the issues around boys' achievement with parents. Particularly important is to encourage male family members to engage with their boy's education. Dads need to know, for example, that by being involved in their boys' education they significantly increase the chances of their boys' achieving and forming positive relationships. It is well understood that they need to read to their children, and also to share the joy of reading themselves, so that reading is not perceived as something only females do.

Bonus Idea ★

Create the opportunity for a parents' workshop day, when small groups are taught a range of skills in workshops run by parents.

Men behaving dadly 1

"We invited dads in by name – they saw their child in class and it really helped them to see how they could help at home."

Research suggests that a father's positive involvement in his son's upbringing will have a direct impact on the boy's education.

The term 'dads' here is taken to include all male carers, including stepfathers and extended family members such as granddads, uncles, older male siblings, etc.

Research suggests that a father's positive involvement in his son's upbringing will have a direct impact on a boy's education, future success with relationships and avoidance of criminal activity, and this is regardless of whether the father is living at home or not. Yet too often school matters are seen as the mother's concern.

Boys need positive older male role models within the close or extended family, and this, it might be argued, is especially true where there is a significant lack of male teachers in primary schools. However, involving dads can be difficult.

Countless projects across the country have proved that there are four main keys to success.

- Address dads directly – general letters to parents usually end up with mum and/or fail to engage dads.
- Give dads plenty of notice of any events or activities you'd like them to attend.
- Sometimes it can help to choose 'male-friendly' activities, e.g. in one school a group of dads met on a Saturday morning with their children to make a rowing boat from a kit. Other projects have included rocket building, reading clubs and model-making clubs.
- It can be very useful to encourage mums to encourage dads to get involved!

Teaching Tip

Advance notice has been identified as an issue for dads, but sometimes spontaneous action can bear fruit! Why not ask any dads who regularly bring boys into school whether they would like to stay for half an hour to help in school?

Taking it Further

Make 'Male role models in the school community' an agenda item on your next staff, governors and PTA meeting. Have a 'Men Behaving Dadly' noticeboard for news and information.

Men behaving dadly 2

"It was an honour to be asked." A dad, having been asked to pose for a poster to encourage other dads to read to their child.

Engaging males from the close and extended family in school is not always easy. However, some schools have been successful, and those schools often share the same basic steps.

Teaching Tip

Create posters of dads, granddads, etc. reading to their children and display around the school.

Have special events in school to celebrate Father's Day and Grandfather's Day.

Step 1: Invite dads in!

Create specific events that provide an opportunity for dads to come into school, e.g. a 'Bring a dad to school' day. Send out letters directly to the chosen dads (or other relatives), giving them plenty of advance notice. The dads could work in class with their child or talk to the class about their lives, their work, their hobbies.

One school successfully recruited a number of dads, older brothers, uncles and granddads to run workshops for small groups of boys, utilising their available skills. One older brother delivered a DJ'ing workshop, whilst a dad delivered a cookery workshop, and one granddad delivered an origami workshop.

Step 2: Make dads feel welcome!

Give dads and male carers a visual presence around the school.

Step 3: Get dads involved!

Begin with a simple activity, like playing a game or reading with boys, and later on you could get them involved in a bigger project, if they seem willing.

One school developed a model-making club for dads and their boys to work together in school, another a Warhammer club, and another a book club.

FUDGE (Friends, uncles, dads, grandads, everyone!)

"Me and my dad learnt how to cook together in school today."

Here are some of the ways schools have managed to engage males from the close and extended family at home.

Of course, engaging dads and males in the close and extended family is also important at home. Lancashire SureStart supply activity sacks to loan to boys and their dads/male carers, with titles such as 'Explorer' and 'Builder', which include stories, non-fiction reference material and a variety of objects.

Dads/male carers should also be encouraged to generate and share their own ideas. For example, the Limelight Children and Fathers group in Lewisham prepared a booklet of ideas called 'For Dads and Lads'. This includes detailed instructions for things to do together such as:

- scientific experiments
- make a meal
- make a bird feeder
- make a kite
- visit a library
- go on a wildlife hunt
- follow a museum trail.

Teaching Tip

Produce your own explorer, builder, wildlife detective, etc. packs. Encourage fathers/carers and sons to keep a diary of their project together.

Taking it Further

You might even consider arranging an event where participants present their projects to other dads and granddads. When planning such an event, firstly put yourself in a dad's shoes – would they feel welcome? What could we do to make sure they feel really welcome? Make it fun but make it purposeful and valuable too!

Positive male role models in the school community

"Those little boys really look up to the big boys."

We need to find and engage with positive male role models wherever we can.

Many would say that if only we had more male teachers in primary schools the problem would be solved. The proportion of the teaching profession that is male and under the age of thirty in both primary and secondary schools is less than 5%. So it is just as well that it is not the gender of the teacher that is the most important thing. It is the quality of the teacher, and when it comes to boys it is about a teacher's ability to link into what it is that's going on in a boy's head, in a boy's world, in a boy's universe. That said, clearly it would be beneficial to boys to find and utilise positive male role models in whatever way we can.

- Ask your local high school if they could provide a group of Year 9 or 10 boys to counsel Year 6s on life in high school.
- Whilst high schools often tend to offer boys to coach football or basketball as part of their junior sports leadership courses, it may also be useful to have the older boys as ambassadors for academic subjects, and offer tutorials to younger students.

Consider the case of one Year 6 boy helping with Year 1. The younger of the two was misbehaving and went under his table to escape trouble. The older asked if he could 'try and sort him', which he promptly and peacefully did with the quiet aside 'look what you can do instead of trouble and mischief!'

Gender stereotyping

Part 7

Investigate and challenge gender stereotypes

"I want two strong boys to fetch me a table."

Gender stereotyping is rife in society, and it begins in nursery with boys telling other boys 'You can't wear that you're a boy!'

Teaching Tip

Engage your class in research into masculine and feminine gender stereotyping. Toy catalogues are a good place to start.

Taking it Further

Ask your local high school if they have boys that might be able to provide drama or music presentations or workshops, or act as reading buddies.

Bonus Idea ★

Get your class to write letters to toy manufacturers, shops or authors expressing their concerns.

The following examples will help you to begin to address gender stereotypes with children.

- Read books to the children that portray gender stereotypes and provide time for discussion afterwards. Did the children recognise the stereotype? How does it relate to their own experience? Do they think these stereotypes are fair?
- Challenge your class to find books that show males in a positive light (it's harder than you think!).
- Discuss common figures of speech, such as: 'Boys will be boys!', 'Are you man enough?', 'Just the man for the job!', 'Real men don't cry'. What do these sayings mean? Are they fair?
- Explore catalogues showing children's toys and clothing, and discuss the stereotypes to which they cater.
- Collect and share advertisements from magazines or the television that show males in a negative light.
- Pose questions for the children to consider as a group. Can anyone be a hero? What do we mean when we say someone is strong? Can a person be tough and tender at the same time?
- Introduce the children to people who break out of 'stereotypical' roles (e.g. at work).

Genderwatch!
The way forward!

"Let's keep gender on the agenda!"

Having aroused their interest in gender stereotyping, children need channels through which to express their feelings. Here are just a few suggestions. They will think of more!

Step 1

Discuss the outcomes of the class research.

Step 2

Set up a series of role play situations in pairs, where one pupil is lodging a complaint about gender stereotyping in clothing, toy catalogues, TV advertising etc.

Step 3

Get your class to write a letter expressing their points of view to appropriate offenders.

Step 4

Make a class film to send to the offending company.

Step 5

Phone up relevant customer relations departments. You could audition/rehearse this first with the class.

Step 6

Get your class to present a school assembly based on their findings. Think about including role plays as well as any responses they have received from letters and phone calls.

Taking it Further

Create and maintain a 'Genderwatch' noticeboard, where the class can post any news items, book titles, advertisements, etc. Keep the debate alive!

Gendered behaviour – the way forward for teachers

"You can't wear that, you're a boy!"

The good news is that gendered behaviour is learnt, and if it's learnt it can be unlearnt.

It's easy for gender imbalance in groups and activities, gender stereotyping and gender bias in resources to pass us by. It is important that we take time out to explore these as a group of colleagues and address any issues that arise.

- Think carefully about the tasks given to boys and the tasks given to girls, whether it's moving furniture, helping out at parents' sessions, cooking at school fairs, or caring for younger children in the playground.
- Ensure there is a gender balance amongst peer befrienders, playground buddies, play leaders, librarians, members of the school council.
- Reflect on whether your school honours the tender feelings of boys (banning 'man up' would be a start).
- Reflect on whether your school rewards and celebrates acts of kindness.
- Ensure that there is a gender balance in displays of work, in the entrance hall, on the corridor, on the school website, in the classroom.
- Ensure that there is a gender balance in library books, classroom materials, role play areas.
- Think carefully about how you talk to boys and how you talk to girls (see Idea 44).

Your school could help by challenging gender stereotypes right from the start, for example, "You can't wear that, you're a boy!"

Gender issues in school: take a health check

"We can't stand by and watch generation after generation of boys being told by other boys what kind of boys they need to be"

Engage your class on research on peer pressure based on gender stereotyping.

At one primary school, whilst I was delivering a twilight session for staff I could see out of the corner of my eye a yoga lesson going on in the hall. I commented to the staff how much I loved to see yoga in schools.

Yoga is cross-cultural, non-competitive and it can clearly help to get youngsters in the right emotional state for learning. What's more, it can help to ameliorate the negative impact of the macho nature of the wider community that's trying to seep in through the doors, the windows and the very fabric of the building (see idea 41). A cursory glance at any set of statistics about children in the UK (e.g. UNICEF 2012) suggests that our children are desperately in need of such tools that could positively impact on their wellbeing.

On this particular occasion I noticed that there weren't any boys in the group. I asked if there were different yoga sessions for boys and girls. 'No, it's for everybody.' 'But...er, there are no boys.' 'There used to be.' And at that point she gestured towards a boy in the corner. 'My son used to come. But he got so much stick from his mates, he stopped.'

Clearly the peer police had been allowed to determine what other boys do, and the lack of discussion or action had made it worse. That's why it's so important to explore any examples of gender imbalance in your school.

Teaching Tip

Explore as a staff the make up of groups, displays of youngsters achieving, or pupils' work.

Taking it Further

Look up YogaBugs and Relax Kids for more details on yoga training.

Peer pressure

Part 8

Peer pressure

"Shooting themselves in the foot."

Peer pressure is one of the most significant barriers to boys' achievement. So what are we doing about it? What can we do?

Teaching Tip

Following a discussion of these points, invite boys to create a piece of role play about the issue, and show it in assembly.

In discussion, identify the 'peer police' in your school. These are the boys who:

- police the boundaries of what they consider to be gender-appropriate behaviour; they want other boys to conform to their ways of thinking and their ways of working (or not as the case may be!)
- have natural leadership ability which they use to tease other boys who like to work hard, read, sing, dance, show their feelings or celebrate success
- are 'peer influencers' – boys follow their lead.

What are you and your colleagues doing to nip the issue of peer pressure in the bud? What works? What doesn't?

Be alert to peer interaction. Make a point, throughout the school, of informally commenting on and rewarding supportive behaviour as it occurs. Make sure that your school regularly rewards supportive peer behaviour.

- Ask boys to list all the benefits of working hard and then all the benefits of allowing others to tell them not to work hard – let them draw their own conclusions!
- Introduce the saying 'Shoot yourself in the foot'. Ask boys what it means and how it applies to the problem of peer pressure.
- Encourage them to think of different ways to express this concept, and use their ideas to create a poster campaign to tackle the problem of peer pressure.

Taking it Further

Use the tried and tested approaches described in Ideas 77 and 78.

Dealing with peer pressure

"It's a tough call turning up first day at the high school with a violin case if you're a boy."

We need to tackle peer pressure from the earliest opportunity and address related issues constantly.

Geek, nerd, neek, swot, spoff, spoffboff, boffin, keener, keeno, square, squarebear, teacher's pet, stew, sook... the list is endless!

Boys seem to be much more sensitive to certain types of peer pressure than girls. Peer pressure starts in the nursery, and by the time some boys reach Year 6 they are already creating difficulties for other boys, who are sometimes torn between friendships and the desire to get on and learn.

In virtually all primary schools, in my experience, there is a small group of boys in Year 6 who have a negative influence on other boys. By Year 10 in secondary school, these boys, the fully fledged peer police, can effectively be described as running the school. They are the ones who are telling other boys whether it's okay to care to share, to feel, to work, to dance, to sing, to write, to read, virtually everything.

Of all the barriers to boys' achievement, peer pressure can be *the* most significant for so many boys. In Year 11, as they face their exams, the boys frequently regret not having been more of a 'swot' and wish they had been less influenced by peer pressure.

It's a huge problem, but there are positive approaches to tackling it. A combination of humour, discussion and opportunities to channel natural leadership ability are all effective ways of dealing with peer pressure.

Teaching Tip

Appeal to boys' sense of the ridiculous by heaping ridicule upon peer pressure, and cutting the problem down to size. Use the following poem as a stimulus for discussion in a P4C session and/or for a school assembly:

You keep calling me a swot / You call me prof / You keep calling me crawler / You call me boff / You keep calling me a nerd / You call me a geek / You keep calling me brainbox / You call me creep. One thing's clear, you're not so bright, YOU... can't even get my name right! By Gary Wilson

P4C, Philosophy for Children, is a tool that can be used with great effect to help develop thinking and communication skills (see sapere.org.uk)

Dealing with the peer police 1

"Has it changed him, being a transformer? Aye, he were a right little git before he was a transformer, couldn't get him out of bed. Now he can't wait to get here!"

Give the peer leaders a positive focus for their natural leadership ability and see them turn around!

Teaching Tip

You could ask your peer leaders to:

- help younger ones with reading
- support play in Early Years
- work as playground buddies
- promote reading (pictures or posters of them reading can send powerful messages)
- take on significant responsibilities around school.

Taking it Further

Develop your own transformer scheme incorporating elements of the list above. To work with groups in other schools can create even greater benefits. See Idea 19.

Several years ago, whilst involved in a local project in Bradford with 25 primary schools, I asked at the launch if any of them had a small group of boys in Year 6 who were a negative influence on the other boys, trying to 'drag them off a cliff'. The response was almost unanimous: yes, they did. I have discovered over the years that most primary schools have such a group, maybe not in every cohort, but the problem is clearly extensive.

In one of the initial project schools, the head told me about a particular boy in her school called Jack. Jack and one or two of his friends taunted other boys because they worked hard. Their behaviour generally was detrimental to everyone's learning.

I recommended that she give Jack and his friends a positive focus for their natural leadership ability. (The clue is in the title, they are peer *leaders*.) The head teacher approached them and offered them a very special role: to lead a fundraising campaign to help boys in their twin school in South America.

Jack immediately offered to do a sponsored BMX ride around the playground. He raised a considerable amount of money, but more importantly, he raised his profile in a positive way; from that moment on, Jack began to drag boys up the mountain, instead of dragging them over the cliff!

Positive labelling, as all parties agreed, was part of the reason for the plan's success. On my recommendation the head teacher gave the group a name: 'The Transformers'. The school now regularly operates a 'transformer scheme'. (Jack later competed in international BMX competitions and is now one of the best BMX riders in the world in his age group. The school didn't even know about his BMX riding!).

Many schools and some local authorities that I have worked with have successfully channelled this natural leadership ability by giving it a positive focus, creating their own transformer scheme.

Do it! It really works.

Dealing with the peer police 2 – go large!

"Transformers? They loved that name."

Giving peer leaders a positive focus changes a lot of boys' attitudes towards themselves, their learning and school.

Teaching Tip

Develop your own 'transformers' scheme, along the lines of the model presented here.

a) Identify the peer leaders,
b) Give them the opportunity to express their natural leadership ability in a positive way by giving them the opportunity to succeed in a given task
c) Follow this up by giving the group a regular chance to contribute positively to the life of the school
d) Celebrate their achievements in a very public way.

Taking it Further

Organise your transformers scheme alongside other schools so that you can set up visits of other transformers and ultimately hold a conference to celebrate their achievements too!

A project I led across the London Borough of Bexley involved 25 primary schools. Each school identified a small group of usually between three and five boys in their Year 6 classes who were negative peer leaders. I recommended that we try a 'transformers' scheme to work across all the schools in the authority. The boys were informed that they were key members of the school population who were singled out for their particular skills and would be, during the course of the year, given significant roles and responsibilities including:

- helping out in nursery and reception from time to time
- running eco-friendly projects in school
- taking responsibilities for visitors
- helping at school functions
- working as mentors for younger boys
- meeting with transformers from other schools in their area to discuss their plans and their successes.

At the end of the year all of the transformers (almost a hundred in total) met together in a conference with their head teachers to celebrate their achievements. The conference included a number of motivational speakers and presentations, including presentations from the boys themselves.

It had a major positive impact in a variety of ways.

- It raised the profile of the boys in a positive way by giving them a positive focus for their natural leadership ability (the clue is in the title 'Peer Leaders').
- It changed a lot of boys' attitudes towards themselves by increasing their sense of self-worth.
- It changed a lot of teachers' attitudes towards those boys, even those who had never taught them, but had just heard them regularly complained about in the staffroom. As a result of this work the boys' motivation significantly improved. One local high school also became involved when it identified a small group of peer leaders in Year 10 and trained them up as maths and science ambassadors to work with Year 6s in their feeder primaries.

Labelling boys

Part 9

We say the craziest things!

"Treat people as if they are what they ought to be and you can help them to become what they are capable of being." Goethe

Negative labelling starts in the home. What can we do?

Teaching Tip

Discuss as a staff these examples and other examples of labelling that you have all encountered or, indeed, suffered yourself!

- Introducing her son on the first day, a mum hands him over, saying, within earshot of the boy, 'He's a right little terror!'

What would your reaction be to that?

On the other hand, have you ever heard anyone say anything like the following?

- Teacher greeting a boy for the first time into her class: 'So, you're Sarah's brother are you? Are you as clever as your sister?'
- Teacher at a parents' evening, greeting the boy with parents: 'Hello trouble!' Mother responds: 'Is my son trouble?' 'Why, er...no'. 'Then please don't call him that!'
- Teacher in a staffroom talking about 'that class': 'What do you expect from that lot?'
- Teacher greeting a supply teacher: 'That lot will lead you a merry dance.'
- Advice to a teacher at the start of a new school year (the boy was in Reception): 'You're going to have to get that one onside.'
- 'Residential? I wouldn't take that lot to the end of the street!'

Taking it Further

Discuss negative labelling with your class. See Idea 81.

Positive labels

"Never mind boys will be boys...Boys will be BRILLIANT"

Because the negative labelling of boys is so all pervading, even as professionals we can get drawn into it sometimes.

Gender labels, however affectionately meant, can have a serious effect on self-esteem and confidence. Consider t-shirts with slogans such as 'Boys are stupid – throw rocks at them', 'I'm a little monster', or toddler clothing sold under gendered brand names, such as 'Sweet Millie' (for girls) or 'Scruff' (for boys).

It's easy to be drawn into this kind of labelling. It may be upsetting to think that we could be labelling boys in this way ourselves, as we love teaching boys! We love the way they get so enthusiastic when we grab them with something that excites and engages them, we love the fact they like taking risks, we love their openness, their sense of humour, their sense of fun. We love the fact that they can be a little bit more challenging because that makes it more rewarding! We also love the fact that every day is a new day for them!

Negative labels, once applied, are often very hard to remove. We need to make a conscious effort to identify negative labelling, to avoid using it ourselves, and to question it with our pupils.

Get your class to research, collect and explore examples of products similar to those described above. Ask them, 'How do the slogans and catchphrases make you feel? How might they make others feel?' Explore TV advertisements that show negative gender stereotypes.

> **Taking it Further**
>
> Get the class to write to the companies saying what they feel about the negative stereotypes.

Labels really stick

"I know all about you, son, you can sit over there."

The smallest thing we say to a child can stay with them for a very long time.

Teaching Tip

Together create new, positive labels about boys'. Get them to design and display posters to encourage boys to 'think positive!'.

I was invited to have a discussion with a group of 15 teenage boys in a high school. They looked miserable as they came in and as one boy walked past me he said, 'We're the 15 worst boys in school, sir'. When I asked him what made him think that, he replied, 'The principal, sir, he just told us.'

I suggested that we got a message back to the principal: 'what school has been like for us'. During that hour, and many, many subsequent hours, I heard stories of boys who've felt they had a reputation they just couldn't shift. They'd wanted to do better, and had walked in full of optimism, and the teacher had said, 'I know all about you, son...you can sit over there.'

When I told the teachers at their twilight session, one teacher recounted the story of his first day at school. He was faced with a big sheet of blank paper and some paints. He had no idea what to do, then decided that he'd paint the whole sheet red. The teacher came along the row and praised everyone's efforts until they got to his, and said disdainfully, 'Martin, you're going to be just like your father, the decorator'. He recalled that mentally and physically he just slumped. It wasn't until a couple of years later that he finally picked himself up, when a supply teacher taught them all how to do 3D drawings; he did a passable interpretation of a kennel and she held it up as exemplary.

Taking it Further

Never say 'Boys will be Boys!' again. *Ever*. Have a new style version of a swear box in the staffroom; every time a colleague uses a gender stereotypical phrase, it costs them!

Am I brilliant today or am I fantastic?

"You can't sing, you can sit down. Just stand at the back, love, and mime."

There is no doubt that both positive and negative labels stick and become part of our image of ourselves or of others.

Once, whilst talking to a teacher in a primary school, a young boy came up and asked, 'am I brilliant today or am I fantastic, miss?' Immediately she responded, 'You're fantastic love'. When I asked why, she explained, 'Oh that, that's nothing, it's just that I have different groups for different activities and I used to label them different fruit or different colours...'.

In a staff meeting, ask about their experience of labelling. Try this: 'How many of you, when you were at school, were asked to stand up and sing a few notes, and if the teacher thought you could sing they would say 'yes, you can sing' and if you couldn't then they said, ' You can't sing, you can sit down'. Undoubtedly this will have happened to some of your colleagues – now ask them if they've sung since. You'll be amazed.

There is no doubt that both positive and negative labels stick. A teacher told me when I was nine that I could write poetry. I've been writing poetry ever since. So how about we start creating more positive labels? Today the class... tomorrow the world!

• The terrible two's! = The terrific two's!

Do you know that in Ireland they call Early Years the Incredible Years?

Teaching Tip

Give the different groups in your class brand new titles: The Fantastic Group, The Brilliant Group, the Awesome Group.

Taking it Further

Rename your Early Years 'The Incredible Years'.

So what do you expect?

"Well, he's a lad, what do you expect?"

Do we have the same high expectations of boys and girls?

Teaching Tip

Note when a boy that you are concerned about comes out with something that surprises you. Sometimes they do come out with the most amazing things and you think 'Where on earth has he got that from?'

Celebrate those moments publicly and remind him regularly what he is capable of.

As professionals we are aware that not all boys underachieve. Statistically, it is clear that more often than not it does tend to be poor, white working class boys at the bottom of the heap, although it is not exclusively the case. It should go without saying that this knowledge should not lead to a lowering of expectations. We need to have the highest expectations of all boys and all girls. In our work to help boys and girls to achieve, the last thing we would wish for is for boys to feel that we have low expectations of their levels of achievement. A staff discussion along the following lines could prove most useful.

- Do all adults in the classroom, in the playground and in the dining hall, have the same high expectations of boys' and girls' behaviour?
- Do all adults respond in a consistent fashion to boys and girls over misdemeanours?
- Do all adults in the classroom have the same high expectations of boys and girls with regard to their attitude to work?
- Do all adults in the classroom have the same high expectations of boys and girls with regard to their performance in all subjects?
- Do you ever see examples of boys and girls having low expectations of themselves? Lacking self-belief?
- Do you regularly remind all pupils that you have belief in them?
- Are all pupils aware that you care about their effort, progress and happiness?
- What can be done in response to any of the above?

Taking it Further

Create a 'Where did they get that from!' display in the staffroom to share their successes with everyone.

Getting boys on the agenda (a quick strategic approach)

Part 10

Getting boys on the agenda 1

"I just love their enthusiasm when I present them with something that really engages them!"

We need to begin by sharing our thoughts on the successes we already have with boys so that we start from our own strengths. The next few ideas outline a series of three staff meetings to work on raising boys' achievement in your school.

Teaching Tip

Brainstorm all the positive aspects of teaching boys. Use the following ideas to get you started.

I like teaching boys because...

- They can be really enthusiastic when something catches their imagination.
- They can be challenging and therefore rewarding.
- They are often open and honest.

The best way to start any project is to consider what is already known or in place. Begin your own school's project to get the best out of boys by focusing on the positive: your successes with boys. Together, you can:

- explore your perceptions of boys' achievement and your attitudes towards boys
- raise your own awareness by sharing the experiences of colleagues
- use your findings to provide valuable information on the best way forward.

A series of three staff meetings should help you to get the ball rolling.

Staff Meeting 1 Identifying your strengths

Too often, we find ourselves drawn into the negative labelling of boys that appears endemic in today's society. Focusing on what we appreciate about boys' characteristics as learners can be a positive way of starting the process of raising our expectations, as well as their achievement and self-esteem.

Base the meeting around thought-provoking questions that focus on the successes staff have had with boys. Steer clear of negativity!

Getting boys on the agenda 2: Next steps

"I've seen success with boys when...."

Beginning work on raising boys' achievement means first and foremost recognising what it is that we already do that brings about success with boys.

Staff Meeting 1 continued Identifying your successes.

Share together as a staff your own experiences and examples of when you have seen success with boys (you may like to discuss what you mean by 'success' first). Encourage everyone to talk only in positive terms. Discuss the following questions.

- What, in your opinion, brings about success with boys?
- What kinds of activities have you found engage boys best?
- Which of the topics that you have covered do boys seem to enjoy best?
- What material do you find is particularly popular with boys?
- What approaches have brought about success in boys?
- Do we regularly show boys how much we love teaching them?
- Do we regularly show boys how much we value their contribution?

End the discussion by compiling a list of your successful approaches, materials and activities. These should be areas for you to capitalise on as a starting point for your boys' project.

Your research with boys, in preparation for Staff Meeting 2 (see Idea 87), will undoubtedly serve to further enhance your list of how to achieve even more success.

Teaching Tip

Here are some examples to start you off. I have seen success when I've...

- given them lots of praise and encouragement
- let them take the lead in a lesson
- used particular resources such as visual media, books or artefacts
- used a particular approach such as role play, group work or working with partners
- taken them outside the classroom environment
- made learning fun.

Let's hear it from the boys

"I'm not a boys' expert, I'm a boys' champion. Ask them what you want to know; they're the experts."

The voices of the boys need to be heard from the beginning of the project.

Taking it Further

Adapt the list of starters to suit the needs of your pupils (this list is probably more suitable for Year 4 and up). You could make up your own list of questions entirely, of course! The only thing that matters is that the voices of the boys are heard in the second meeting.

Preparing for Staff Meeting 2

Boys – we want to hear from you!
Before this meeting, encourage staff to carry out their own research. Ask them to:

- Collect and compare data from across the school on boys' and girls' achievements and attitudes, e.g. boys' performance across subjects, behaviour logs, motivation and attitude scores, number of books borrowed from the library, awards, merits, credits etc.
- Consider what this data reveals about boys' achievement and attitudes.
- Ask the experts. Talk to the boys and find out what engages them in school and learning.

Use the starters below as a starting point for interviewing individual boys:

- The best type of activities we do in lessons are...
- The best piece of work I've ever done is...
- When the teacher praises my work I feel...
- When my teacher reads my work out in class I feel...
- When I am given a presentation in assembly I feel...
- The best kinds of books are...
- What really helps me with my writing is when...
- What really gets in the way of my learning is...
- I know that I could really improve my work if...
- The best way of being rewarded for good work is...
- When my teacher talks about my handwriting I feel...
- Any further comments.

So what do we know already?

"We can be really bad as a profession at sharing thoughts and ideas, unlike in medicine where it is considered hugely important." Ted Wragg.

Draw up a list of barriers to boys' achievement as identified by all staff. What do *you* think is preventing some boys from achieving well? You will find more in Idea 89.

Staff Meeting 2 Sharing research.

The focus of this meeting is to share the action research following Meeting 1 and to draw up a list of barriers to boys' learning. If appropriate, prior to Meeting 2, staff from different key stages may want to collate results. (There may be a lot of data to go through!)

Discuss and note down all the issues affecting boys' underachievement in your school and identify areas where the school could improve its approach to the problem.

Break these down into general whole-school and more specific year group issues. For example, a whole-school issue could be lack of parental involvement, where a specific issue could be that Year 6 boys seem to suffer more from peer pressure.

Taking it Further

Collate some initial thoughts on how the situation may be improved.

Meeting 2: Barriers

"You can't tackle all of this at once!"

Compile a comprehensive list of barriers and start to prioritise which barriers you need to begin addressing first.

Teaching Tip

Before the next meeting, you may want to get together in year groups to discuss your ideas.

In addition to the barriers you have discovered yourself you might like to consider some of the examples listed below.

Whole school barriers to boys' learning:

- lack of, or ineffective, communication between teachers and boys
- lack of parental involvement
- negative attitude towards reading and/or writing
- lack of opportunity for reflective work
- low teacher expectations
- mismatch of teaching and learning styles to boys' preferred ways of working
- lack of male role models in school.

Specific barriers to boys' learning:

- low self-esteem
- lack of independence skills
- limiting self-beliefs
- low levels of motivation
- poorly developed fine motor skills
- poor speaking and listening skills
- onset of peer pressure
- emotional intelligence issues
- 'laddish' behaviour.

Taking it Further

For a more comprehensive list of barriers to boys' achievement, see *Breaking Through Barriers to Boys' Achievement and Developing a Caring Masculinity*, G. Wilson, Bloomsbury Publishing PLC. You will also find many tried and tested strategies here.

After discussing your own research findings and considering the barriers listed above, decide which are your top three whole-school priorities, and three priorities that apply specifically to your class. You will then need to start thinking of strategies to tackle these top three priorities.

Where do we go from here?

"You can't target all the barriers at once."

Prioritise action for individual classes, and also prioritise which barriers require action for whole school.

Staff Meeting 3 Making a plan.

Now you have identified your top three barriers to boys' learning and have had some time to think about strategies to address these, you will need to get together and draw up a plan.

Recap on the previous meeting, focusing on the top three barriers you identified.

You can now begin to make action plan, one for the whole school and one for your class, by filling in your strategy charts. Use the following headings:

- Barrier to boy's learning – a short description of the barrier
- Priority in order of importance (1 to 5)
- Strategies to remove barrier
- Who is responsible?
- Timescale

Taking it Further

Explore *Breaking Through the Barriers to Boys' Achievement* and *Raising Boys' Achievement – Pocket Pal*, G. Wilson, Bloomsbury Publishing PLC.

Staff meeting 3 continued

"The 'I's have it' model."

This model provides a quick, low-cost approach to innovation that requires little in terms of resources or time

The 'I's have it' model gives a framework you can use to move your strategies forward. The model below offers a process for implementing change in your school. Why not try it out?

Prompt, positive and thorough feedback will be vital to the long-term success of your project. For example, in the case of specific barriers, individual teachers could be initially encouraged to take on board one initiative that feels pertinent to them.

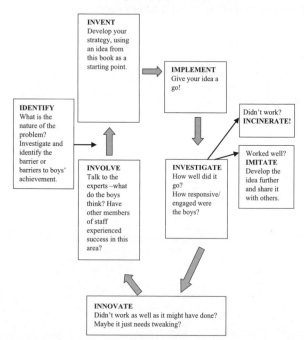

INVENT
Develop your strategy, using an idea from this book as a starting point.

IMPLEMENT
Give your idea a go!

IDENTIFY
What is the nature of the problem? Investigate and identify the barrier or barriers to boys' achievement.

INVOLVE
Talk to the experts –what do the boys think? Have other members of staff experienced success in this area?

INVESTIGATE
How well did it go? How responsive/ engaged were the boys?

Didn't work?
INCINERATE!

Worked well?
IMITATE
Develop the idea further and share it with others.

INNOVATE
Didn't work as well as it might have done? Maybe it just needs tweaking?

Staff meeting 3 continued

"How did we do?"

How well have your strategies worked? Ask yourself, your in-class support and your boys (and girls)!

Keep a record of any strategies that you implement. This will help you to compare and monitor their effectiveness. The following headings will help you organise your results:

- Target group – was the strategy intended for a small group of boys? All boys? The whole class?
- Strategy
- What specific problem did you focus on? Where did you get the idea?
- How well did it go? Ask the boys for their opinions as well as giving your own.
- Any modifications necessary?
- Colleagues may have ideas as to how the strategy might be modified

Teaching Tip

Set up a 'Brilliant boys' project noticeboard in the staffroom where you can display short summaries of strategies that have worked. Include on the noticeboard any comments from boys (and girls) about any innovations.

Include a regular five-minute slot in weekly staff meetings for individual members of staff to give quick feedback on successful innovations.

Checklists and quick tips

Part 11

A quick checklist for primary teachers in a hurry

"Are some of our boys achieving less well than the girls? Is it all their fault? What could we do?"

Are we providing the kind of opportunities for learning that actively engage boys?

Teaching Tip

Do a quick personal audit on as many of these points as you feel you can on your own. Then, as a team, discuss the questions. Are you lacking in any respect? Which might you prioritise for action, as a team/practitioner?

Taking it Further

Consider which of the questions on the list might be appropriate to ask the boys. Then ask them!

Bonus Idea ★

Actively involve boys in the planning of activities that will engage them. What might we reasonably expect parents to do to help?

Sometimes just whizzing through a checklist might be all we need to remind ourselves of the need to take action, and sometimes it might just unearth some fundamentally important points that we've never even thought about in order to get it right for the boys as they work their way through primary school. Are we addressing the following?

- Do we plan experiences for boys that relate to their interests and enthusiasms?
- Do we involve them in the planning of activities that they will engage with?
- Do we show boys that we value their interests as much as the interests of girls?
- Would we be able to see that by just glancing around the classroom?
- Do the resources in the room provide equally for boys' and girls' interests (e.g. reading and role-play areas)?
- Do we monitor the numbers of rewards and sanctions handed out to boys and girls?
- Do we ensure that we do not stereotype by gender?
- Do we sometimes mistake boys' behaviour as naughtiness when actually it is sheer enthusiasm?
- Do we see boys as annoying or just curious?
- Do we see boys as loud or enthusiastic?
- Do boys appear to be desperately challenging or desperately in need of a challenge?

- Do we encourage girls and boys to talk about what is troubling them?
- Do we know enough about boys' interests, strengths and preferred ways of learning?
- Do we value what it is that boys bring to the table and the contributions they make?
- Does the whole school share the same views on the learning needs of boys and how to address them?
- Do we all share the same high expectations of all girls and all boys?
- Do we ask all of our children open ended questions or do we just ask the girls?

Quick tips for teachers in a hurry

"There's no such thing as a quick fix but sometimes just a tweak can make all the difference."

With regard to the issue of boys' underachievement, there isn't just a single reason why some of our boys fail to achieve. Neither is there a simple solution.

Teaching Tip

For the full picture see *Breaking Through the Barriers to Boys' Achievement*, which outlines in detail the thirty or so barriers and offers a variety of strategies to help in the classroom and numerous models for schools to move the raising boys' achievement agenda forward.

There is no quick fix and this book certainly does not set out to be such a thing; it is based upon 23 years' experience of working with the issue and is meant simply to present some simple, practical strategies to try.

Bearing this in mind, there are certain simple, practical things that you can try in the classroom that will make a difference.

- Connecting the learning is particularly important for boys. If they don't see a clear sense and purpose in what they are asked to do, many boys won't engage.
- Give them the big picture. Mapping out ideas using graphic organisers of any kind, from mind maps to fishbone diagrams, can really aid a boy's engagement with learning.
- Create as many opportunities for reflection as you can. For many boys this is the weakest link in their learning process.
- Give boys a system. Checklists, learning mats, and success criteria can really help them.
- Talk, talk, talk and more talk prior to writing.
- For many boys, writing without talking through, discussing, arguing, role playing their ideas first can be a real problem.
- Short-term goals and short-term rewards work best for most boys.

Taking it Further

Make a useful top tips card from the tips on this page and in Idea 95 that you and your in-class support can refer to.

More quick tips for teachers in a hurry

"Make it fun! Make me want to come back to your lesson next time."

Round it up ! Here's a list to get you started, now round it up to ten...or more!

- For boys to function effectively in group work, there needs to be a clear outcome, they need to be grouped effectively and have clear roles and there needs to be an element of challenge.
- Present a challenge the minute they set foot in the room. Problem solving works best.
- The more actively you embrace the Assessment for Learning agenda the better it will be for your boys. It could have been written with just boys in mind – 'Do this, Do that, Get there' – a systematic approach.

Make sure there are some active learning elements in all lessons. Ask yourself: are there enough active learning opportunities in my session, my morning, my day, to ensure that I motivate and engage boys, maintain that engagement and allow them to produce work that is done to the best of their ability?

- Reduce peer pressure by giving peer leaders a positive focus for their natural leadership ability in order to turn them around.
- Reflect on how you talk to boys and how you talk to girls. Look at the frequency, the nature and the quality of those interactions. Many boys believe that teachers prefer girls because of the way we talk to them.

Taking it Further

From your own experience, and as a result of discussions around the content of this book with colleagues and most importantly boys, round this list up to twenty...or more!

11

- Ask the boys! They are the experts. They know what's going wrong for them and they know what they need to do to improve, and what we can do to improve school for them, and above all how, together, we can get it right.
- Make it fun! Relate to their personal interests – value what it is that boys bring to the table.
- Let's help stop the negative labelling that so many boys suffer from. Never mind 'Boys will be boys!' Boys will be brilliant! With your help, if they have self belief and your belief in them, if they have aspirations and we have high expectations of all boys and all girls and we give them just that extra little bit of love.

A few more words from the experts

Part 12

Get it right for the boys 1

"Ask the experts; boys know exactly what is going wrong and what is needed to improve."

How often do we give them the chance to choose the kind of space they'd like to work in?

Develop role play areas right through to the end of Year 6. Not enough space? How about outside? Or part of the hall?

Not enough time? It's a means to an end. Role play is a very powerful tool that helps boys develop their ideas and practice the words they need for writing. It is also a very powerful tool for the social and emotional aspects of learning.

If you're a parent of a boy, have you ever bought him a desk at which you kind of hoped he would sit and do his homework, but he never has? If he'd rather lie on his bed and spread his work out across the bedroom floor, or work at the kitchen table and cover every single surface, don't be surprised, because given half the chance that's the way he'd like to work most of the time.

Invite boys' opinions on:

- The role play corner – is there a gender bias in your role-play corner or do you monitor it carefully?
- Comfortable conditions for working – some ambitious teachers have even engaged children in the design of seating, lighting and sound!
- Wall displays – many boys find busy walls distracting.
- Would a large, single table where they could work collaboratively help boys?

Ask the experts about the working conditions they find most comfortable – the results can be surprising. For example:

- Many teachers report that boys love writing while lying on their tummies.
- Boys tend to work more productively in cooler temperatures.
- Many boys learn more effectively with music – and if there is no music going on, they will make their own! As music doesn't suit everyone, headphones might be a possibility.

Get it right for the boys 2

"The boys will tell you exactly where you are going right and where you are going wrong."

Boys are the experts... ask them what they think.

It's interesting to find out from boys themselves what they like and dislike about school. When asked, they often say they like:

- lessons that involve role play, discussions, group work and working with a friend
- activities that are varied, fun, provide opportunities to work outside and which involve a challenge
- teacher who don't shout at them
- teachers who show an interest in their life out of school
- teachers who treat them fairly
- teachers who set firm boundaries (boys themselves usually recognise that they need boundaries; if they don't have boundaries they can fly off in all kinds of directions)
- teachers who have a sense of fun.

Many boys are motivated by being outdoors. Outdoor activities don't have to be restricted to PE; the key is to think beyond the obvious. Give the boys in your school a say in developing the outdoor environment. They could help design an outdoor:

- storytelling chair
- stage
- work-area with interesting seating arrangements
- learning base – pop-up tents or den-making equipment can provide an exciting new environment for many boys!

Teaching Tip

Ask your boys questions such as:

- what kinds of things make learning interesting?
- what kinds of activity help you to learn best?
- what kind of resources do you like to use?
- what gets in the way of learning?
- what would you like to do more of?
- if there was one thing you'd like to stop doing in school, what would that be?

Obviously you will need to tailor these questions to suit different year groups/pupils.

Taking it Further

After this exercise, discuss with colleagues what they think boys like and dislike about school, then present your findings. Keep the dialogue going!

We did it our way 1

"It's horses for courses, and what works in one school may not always work in another."

It's important to reflect on what works for you, in your own school, as no two schools or even cohorts of children are the same. However, it is always useful to seek out schools where good practice exists and find out exactly what makes them tick.

One school, when asked why they thought their boys achieved at the same level as girls, put together the following list.

- Animals. We have chicks and rabbits and tadpoles and the children look after them from EYFS to Year 6. Boys often become different children when they're talking to the animals.
- We do lots of work on resilience, making sure they understand that we believe that everyone can be successful. We count boys' involvement in Accelerated Reading as an element in this.
- ICT. Every Key Stage 2 child has their own laptop. Not one has been broken in three years.
- Reading awards scheme. From Key Stage 1 onwards all pupils work towards reading awards. When 30 points are accumulated they are taken to a bookshop to choose their own books. A sign of success, we believe, is that every single Year 6 boy is happy to bring a book bag. We expect them to.
- Extracurricular activities are wide ranging and include French, jazz, yoga, gardening and football.

Taking it Further

Share your successes with boys with the rest of your colleagues on a regular basis by making it a regular staff meeting agenda item. Why not? We are talking about roughly half the school population – in fact we're talking about the whole school population, as almost invariably whatever we do for boys has a positive knock-on effect for girls too!

- By the end of Year 6 all pupils will have been on a residential (the Year 6 residential was moved to September to 'get more mileage' and develop relationships with all, but with the slightly more challenging boys in particular).
- We choose curriculum topics, including 'Cornerstones' materials, that have added boy appeal such as *Stargazer*, *Land Ahoy*, *Dinosaurs* and *The Pharaohs*.
- With regard to competition, the focus is on being gracious winners and losers.
- Chess is very big amongst boys. 'They get so engrossed they sometimes almost forget lunch, they love to teach each other and, in a recent school tournament, there were 132 entries.'
- Because of many of the above, boys' attitudes to school and work have shifted significantly.

We did it our way 2

"Go up the front and shine."

This case study shows how Richard Alibon School worked at reflecting boys' interests and developing self-confidence.

Teaching Tip

Invite your class to investigate shared interests. Encourage them to share their expert knowledge with their group and plan a club based on their interests, with membership paraphernalia, advertising to help the club grow, etc. Let their imaginations flow freely. Set aside a time in the week for clubs to meet.

"For the past two years the thrust of our school development plan has been to address the issue of boys' underachievement. This has been achieved through a number of new strategies, schemes and initiatives, but most importantly, a change in mindset from staff. This was initially inspired and lead by Gary Wilson and, as a school, we have worked hard to continue this drive and improve outcomes for boys at our school.

One powerful element of the work was the establishment of a 'Boys' club', initially for the challenging boys in certain year groups, then we targeted free school meals boys. This club runs all year and was offered as a privilege; the boys had to work hard to stay in the club. It ran once a week for an afternoon and the boys had a different focus each half term. We employed a street dancer and the boys produced a dance number they performed to the rest of the school and at the local dance festival. They had a cooking club every week, and learnt how to cook a number of meals that they could go back and cook for their friends and family. We hired a graffiti artist, who designed and developed some graffiti art that is to be painted on school grounds. There is also a sculpture club, storytelling club, and drama club. The boys have all responded incredibly well to these clubs, they enjoy the responsibility and the new skills they are learning, and there have been marked improvements in the behaviour and confidence of the boys that attend."

Taking it Further

Have regular short sessions where club representatives feedback news of the activities of their club to their class.

Frankie, Year 5: 'After doing the performance with the dance group I felt really proud of myself.'

Ephraim, Year 4: 'The boys project gave me confidence, I used to be shy I was glad to be in school because I could make something out of my life.'

Rio, Year 6: 'I feel happy and lucky being part of the dance club and I know my mum is proud of me.'

Harry, Year 6: 'I like that everybody comes together at the drama club and they listen to one another...we say "go up the front and shine", that's what I really like about the sessions.'

Brandon, Year 6: 'What I really like about our storytelling club sessions is listening to stories and getting inspiration.'

Chibuike, Reception: 'I was a superhero and I got to make a superhero sandwich. It made me strong. It was the best, I liked it.'

Boys love teachers who...

"Boys need to know who is in charge — what are the rules and are they being applied consistently?"

Boys are the best barometers of good teachers and good teaching. Ask them what *they* think.

Teaching Tip

Have a discussion around what advice your boys would give younger boys if they're going to do better in school. They might like to produce a leaflet, a film, a report or even a presentation in assembly!

Boys tell me that they love teachers who:

- earn their respect and don't just expect it
- make an effort with them
- treat them equally
- believe in them
- laugh a lot
- are more relaxed
- make learning fun
- don't just talk
- get them to do group work (because the talk helps)
- don't shout
- know what they are talking about.

Above all, boys tell me that they love teachers who are friendly, fun and fair.

One nine year old boy said to me once 'I love teachers who teach with passion!' Boys can also be very aware about what they need to do themselves to improve life in school. Take Harry, a boy who had had a difficult time in primary school and recognised, when he was in Year 6, what he should have done differently in order to have achieved more. He was asked to compile a list of advice for boys. It included:

- don't be distracted by other boys
- don't listen to them if they are trying to put you off or tease you
- concentrate hard in lessons
- don't be worried about putting your hand up
- always be polite and helpful.

Do you know a boy like Harry?

Taking it Further

Harry had some advice for teachers too!

- Think about what it would be like for you as a child.
- Do fun, eventful lessons that make me want to come back for more.
- Let us act out things before we write them.
- Talk to me kindly.
- Don't keep talking about things I did wrong in the past.
- Please don't keep comparing me with my sister.

Ask the experts what advice they might give teachers.